Responsive Design High Performance

Leverage the power of responsive design to fine-tune your website's performance and increase its speed

Dewald Els

BIRMINGHAM - MUMBAI

Responsive Design High Performance

First published: April 2015

Production reference: 1090415

Published by Packt Publishing Ltd.
Livery Place
35 Livery Street
Birmingham B3 2PB, UK.

ISBN 978-1-78439-083-9

www.packtpub.com

Credits

Author

Dewald Els

Reviewers

Younes Baghor (W3bwizart)

Rodrigo Encinas

Evan Mullins

Commissioning Editor

Dipika Gaonkar

Acquisition Editor

Usha Iyer

Content Development Editor

Mohammed Fahad

Neeshma Ramakrishnan

Technical Editor

Narsimha Pai

Copy Editors

Jasmine Nadar

Vikrant Phadke

Project Coordinator

Shweta Birwatkar

Proofreaders

Simran Bhogal

Stephen Copestake

Maria Gould

Indexer

Tejal Soni

Graphics

Sheetal Aute

Disha Haria

Production Coordinator

Manu Joseph

Cover Work

Manu Joseph

About the Author

Dewald Els is short, dark, hairy, and curious. He has extensive experience in PHP and JavaScript. He has worked in the corporate sector after some experience in video game development in C#.

After working in video game development, Dewald joined one of South Africa's top three ISP service providers. He was in the team that developed a solid backend for the ISP from the ground up, to better serve clients. After moving to Pretoria, he currently works for Vane Systems, maintaining their event sales website, `http://www.ticibox.com`. He takes the lead in developing new features for the site.

About the Reviewers

Younes Baghor (W3bwizart) is a freelance lead developer at KBC Touch. He started his career as a welder of trucks and containers and later became a maître d'hôtel. In 2007, he decided to become a programmer, and he graduated in 2010. Although educated in .NET, he was inspired by the Web and HTML5, JavaScript in particular. His experience with web technologies gives him an overall knowledge of the current technologies, libraries, and methodologies driving the modern web today.

Younes is not a guru or expert but knows JavaScript, AngularJS, HTML5, CSS3, mobile-first, progressive enhancement, and responsive design.

Rodrigo Encinas has worked for more than 12 years for companies in different fields, from advertising and television to world-class fashion brands and communication. Nowadays, he works a consultant for international companies, helping them develop web applications and improve user experience with best practices and modern patterns, such as HTML5, responsive web design, and single-page applications.

> I would like to thank Packt Publishing for helping me do a great job, and I would like to thank you for your interest in this field. I would encourage you to learn how to build the Web for the future.

Evan Mullins has always been interested in both design and technology. He studied digital media and earned his BFA degree from the University of Georgia. While attending university, he also studied computer science, animation, and new media. Evan loves the cross-section of art and technology that he finds in the Web.

Professionally, Evan has worked with a slew of start-ups, small businesses, and agencies that build websites: Cartoon Network, Ogilvy & Mather, and Brand Fever. He is currently the lead web developer at Brown Bag Marketing. He is continually busy designing and developing interesting things online.

Since 2004, Evan has maintained a circlecube studio (`http://circlecube.com/2007/01/welcome-to-circle-cube-studio/`), a freelance web studio and playground for open source experiments, examples, and tips that he simply shares as he learns along the way. The blog's content centers on interactive development principles and technologies. He shares what he learns online as well as at conferences.

Evan is happily married and a proud father of four. He enjoys spending time away from work at his real job—his family. He's also busy volunteering for his church and enjoys camping, playing soccer, and playing music.

www.PacktPub.com

Support files, eBooks, discount offers, and more

For support files and downloads related to your book, please visit www.PacktPub.com.

Did you know that Packt offers eBook versions of every book published, with PDF and ePub files available? You can upgrade to the eBook version at www.PacktPub. com and, as a print book customer, you are entitled to a discount on the eBook copy. Get in touch with us at service@packtpub.com for more details.

At www.PacktPub.com, you can also read a collection of free technical articles, sign up for a range of free newsletters, and receive exclusive discounts and offers on Packt books and eBooks.

https://www2.packtpub.com/books/subscription/packtlib

Do you need instant solutions to your IT questions? PacktLib is Packt's online digital book library. Here, you can search, access, and read Packt's entire library of books.

Why subscribe?

- Fully searchable across every book published by Packt
- Copy and paste, print, and bookmark content
- On-demand and accessible via a web browser

Free access for Packt account holders

If you have an account with Packt at www.PacktPub.com, you can use this to access PacktLib today and view 9 entirely free books. Simply use your login credentials for immediate access.

Table of Contents

Preface

Is it responsive? With a growing number of hardware devices that access the web, building a website that is responsive has almost become expected. This can be both good and bad, as responsiveness is a daunting task when not understood properly. So, let's talk about it.

What is responsive design, anyway?

Simply put, a responsive website adapts its layout according to the device being used to access it. The website will dynamically change its layout depending on the device's screen size and orientation.

Some examples of this include menus that collapse, images that resize, and column structures rearranging (for example, a two-column layout converging into one column).

The goal of this book is to make designing and building a website less of a daunting task for the ever-growing number of devices that we use to obtain information from the Internet. We access the Internet from so many different devices, ranging from smart watches to mobile phones and desktops with large high-resolution displays, that responsiveness has become an almost essential feature in web design and development nowadays.

There are prerequisites for a site to qualify as a responsive website. Fluid grids, media queries, and flexible images are a few of them. Additionally, a distinction does need to be made between an *adaptive layout* and a *responsive layout*.

Adaptive Layout

An adaptive layout uses fixed-width grids or columns that are triggered at specific and static points.

Responsive Layout

A responsive website makes use of fluid grids; in other words, the grids resize as the viewport size changes.

What this book covers

Chapter 1, *The Good, the Bad, and the Ugly of Responsive Web Design*, covers what responsive design is and, more importantly, *why* it's so important on the Web today.

Responsive web design helps us create a more uniform appearance across an array of devices. It leaves users feeling more familiar with a brand, regardless of the device they're using to interact with it. Code is kept together in one place, and this negates the need to maintain multiple pages or documents for one website.

Chapter 2, *Tweaking Your Website for Performance*, describes the importance of resource placement on the DOM. It's true that placing scripts at the bottom of the page improves performance, but it's also true that some scripts need to load before the DOM renders.

Preloading content can be greatly helpful in improving the initial load of your site. DNS prefetching is a very helpful piece of code that can resolve the DNS name in the background for the site that your page might point to. Search engines can greatly benefit from this.

Chapter 3, *Managing Images*, proves that managing images is no small feat in a website. Almost all modern websites rely heavily on images to present content to the users.

This chapter explains which image formats to use and when, and also how to optimize your images for websites. We discuss the difference between progressive and optimized images. Conditional loading can greatly help us load our site faster, and we discuss how to use conditional loading to improve our site's performance. We touch on server-side optimization using caches, ETags, and media queries for retina displays.

Chapter 4, Learning Content Management, takes your development in the right direction. We take a look at style sheets, media queries, and how to work with viewports. This chapter also covers the use of CSS preprocessors such as SASSY CSS, SASS, and LESS. Though these are not covered in detail, this serves as an introduction to help you get started. CSS preprocessors are an excellent way to code your style sheets; once you have the hang of it, you can eliminate lines of unnecessary code.

The Web is slowly but surely moving towards an app-like experience, and frameworks such as AngluarJS are right at the forefront of this movement.

This chapter also covers conditional content management with the `<link>` tag to load style sheets based on device size requirements.

Optimization doesn't just occur on the client side, but sometimes on the server side as well, to help deliver correct content before it reaches the client. This is an effective way to manage content.

Parallel downloads are briefly covered. We discuss the fact that the time that the client spends waiting for requests to finish is referred to as blocking, and that our goal should be to reduce blocking as much as possible to achieve shorter load times.

We also cover another excellent way to deliver your sites quickly: by making use of content delivery networks. Then we discuss fonts and how they can affect a website's performance.

Chapter 5, The Fastest HTTP Request is No HTTP Request, proves that one of the best ways to improve the load time of your website is by reducing requests. We look at some effective and easy-to-implement techniques to help you achieve speedy load times. We discuss sprite sheets and how they can take a bunch of requests and turn it into one request. We also provide information about combining files.

Server-side optimization is also a great place to make some improvements. We talk more about server-side optimization and also take a look at AppCache, which is another excellent method to improve your site's performance.

Chapter 6, Testing, Testing, and Testing, asserts that testing is a crucial stage of the development life cycle. It's where you can not only identify problems with your site but also root out performance issues.

Chapter 7, Speeding Up Development with Design Concepts, Patterns, and Programs, focuses on a few ways to improve your site. We kick off by looking at design concepts: graceful degradation, and progressive enhancement. We discuss the differences between these two concepts and how a better user experience can be achieved on a website by making use of progressive enhancement rather than graceful degradation.

Making use of object-oriented CSS (OOCSS) can be a great benefit to your website's maintainability and can improve its loading speed. By following OOCSS, you can reduce the size of your CSS files, thereby improving the download time of the resources required to load your site. We also take a look at how we can improve OOCSS even further by combing it with a CSS preprocessor such as SASS.

There is a brief mention of available patterns to get you started with your project.

Programs such as GruntJS and RequireJS can make you more productive and improve your website's performance. We describe them as well.

Chapter 8, Using Tools for Performance, is basically an introduction. It is intended to point out available applications that you can use to make your development cycle more efficient.

Once we're almost done, we take a look at some resources to take what we've talked about to the next level. We mention some great developers who have made significant contributions to the web field and give you some excellent starting points to further your knowledge of responsive web design.

Appendix, *Taking the Next Steps*, contains an overview of the entire book. It summarizes what we talked about and helps you understand the next steps to becoming a great, responsive web developer.

What you need for this book

This book will focus on improving the performance of your responsive sites. We will go through some exercises to encourage you to think of performance as an integral part of the design process.

At its core, the Web *is* responsive. If you were to create a page with only a few paragraphs of text and a heading or two, you could view that page on any device. The text would automatically reposition itself to fit into any view.

However, as we all know, today's web browsing experience is expected to be much more complex and immersive than a white page with text on it; as we move further into the future of technology, these demands may get bigger and more elaborate. Websites have rich and interactive content, beautiful imagery, interactive elements, and content that spans across wider and wider screens. Along with the complexity of the modern Web, we have seen the arrival of easy-to-use frameworks such as Bootstrap and Foundation to assist with responsiveness; however, even these amazing platforms come with problems of their own, performance being one of the major issues.

In today's immersive, Internet-obsessed world, viewers don't wait longer than a couple of seconds for their content to load, which means that performance is key. We will take a look at principles such as Mobile First, HTTP caching, and dynamic content loading to help make your sites quicker and more responsive, thereby creating an experience that people can enjoy and respond to in a positive way.

Who this book is for

This book is aimed at developers who have experience in building websites and have had at least some exposure to building a responsive website. The goal here is to foster a deeper understanding of responsive websites to improve the way we build them.

You'll need a working knowledge of HTML, CSS3, JavaScript, and jQuery. This book does not provide an introduction to any of these technologies as it assumes that you have moderate knowledge of them.

Conventions

In this book, you will find a number of text styles that distinguish between different kinds of information. Here are some examples of these styles and an explanation of their meaning.

Code words in text, database table names, folder names, filenames, file extensions, pathnames, dummy URLs, user input, and Twitter handles are shown as follows: "As an example, I've included the sizes of the two style sheets from the Bootstrap framework—bootstrap.css and boostrap.min.css."

A block of code is set as follows:

```
<head>
<!-- Styles -->
<link rel="stylesheet" href="css/style.css" type="text/css" />
<!-- Scripts -->
<script src="//ajax.googleapis.com/ajax/libs/jquery/1.11.1/jquery.min.
js"
type="text/javascript" language="Javascript"></script>
</head>
```

When we wish to draw your attention to a particular part of a code block, the relevant lines or items are set in bold:

```
<head>
<!-- Styles -->
<link rel="stylesheet" href="css/style.css" type="text/css" />
<!-- Scripts -->
<script src="//ajax.googleapis.com/ajax/libs/jquery/1.11.1/jquery.min.
js"
type="text/javascript" language="Javascript"></script>
</head>
```

Any command-line input or output is written as follows:

```
npm install -g grunt-cli
```

New terms and **important words** are shown in bold. Words that you see on the screen, for example, in menus or dialog boxes, appear in the text like this: "Clicking on the **Next** button moves you to the next screen."

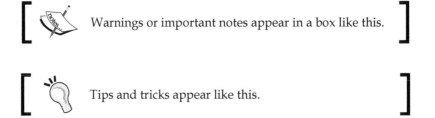

Warnings or important notes appear in a box like this.

Tips and tricks appear like this.

Reader feedback

Feedback from our readers is always welcome. Let us know what you think about this book—what you liked or disliked. Reader feedback is important for us as it helps us develop titles that you will really get the most out of.

To send us general feedback, simply e-mail feedback@packtpub.com, and mention the book's title in the subject of your message.

If there is a topic that you have expertise in and you are interested in either writing or contributing to a book, see our author guide at www.packtpub.com/authors.

Customer support

Now that you are the proud owner of a Packt book, we have a number of things to help you to get the most from your purchase.

Downloading the example code

You can download the example code files from your account at http://www.packtpub.com for all the Packt Publishing books you have purchased. If you purchased this book elsewhere, you can visit http://www.packtpub.com/support and register to have the files e-mailed directly to you.

Downloading the color images of this book

We also provide you with a PDF file that has color images of the screenshots/diagrams used in this book. The color images will help you better understand the changes in the output. You can download this file from: https://www.packtpub.com/sites/default/files/downloads/0839OS_ColoredImages.pdf.

Errata

Although we have taken every care to ensure the accuracy of our content, mistakes do happen. If you find a mistake in one of our books—maybe a mistake in the text or the code—we would be grateful if you could report this to us. By doing so, you can save other readers from frustration and help us improve subsequent versions of this book. If you find any errata, please report them by visiting http://www.packtpub.com/submit-errata, selecting your book, clicking on the **Errata Submission Form** link, and entering the details of your errata. Once your errata are verified, your submission will be accepted and the errata will be uploaded to our website or added to any list of existing errata under the Errata section of that title.

To view the previously submitted errata, go to https://www.packtpub.com/books/content/support and enter the name of the book in the search field. The required information will appear under the **Errata** section.

Piracy

Piracy of copyrighted material on the Internet is an ongoing problem across all media. At Packt, we take the protection of our copyright and licenses very seriously. If you come across any illegal copies of our works in any form on the Internet, please provide us with the location address or website name immediately so that we can pursue a remedy.

Please contact us at `copyright@packtpub.com` with a link to the suspected pirated material.

We appreciate your help in protecting our authors and our ability to bring you valuable content.

Questions

If you have a problem with any aspect of this book, you can contact us at `questions@packtpub.com`, and we will do our best to address the problem.

1
The Good, the Bad, and the Ugly of Responsive Web Design

Responsive web design, often referred to as RWD, has brought many great things for web designers since its inception in 2004, although the term was only coined in 2007 by Ethan Marcotte. The technique of adapting the layout of a site was written by Cameron Adams in 2004.

Here is a breakdown of what we'll discuss in this chapter:

- An overview of the good, the bad, and the ugly of responsive design
- We will look at some examples in each case
- Thereafter, we will take a look at the effects of each example, and how it affects end users and the business

The good – appearance and management

We will be going through the good aspects of responsive web design in the following sections.

Appearance

In appearance, these are the aspects that really stand out:

- **Conformity**: One of the great advantages of responsive web design is the conformity that it brings to our ever-growing, multidevice, browsing experience online. Modern web pages can now easily carry the same design characteristics from desktop to tablet and even to mobile browsers without compromise, thereby greatly enhancing a brand's web presence. Another perk is the ease that this approach brings to code maintenance. In the following screenshot, we can see a good example of adapting a site for multiple devices:

- **User interaction**: Simply changing the site to fit inside different devices is, of course, only the tip of the iceberg. With each change of the layout, the website's usability must remain intact or, in some cases, change to suit the device that it's being viewed on. Here is a good example of user experience staying consistent throughout, from desktop to mobile:

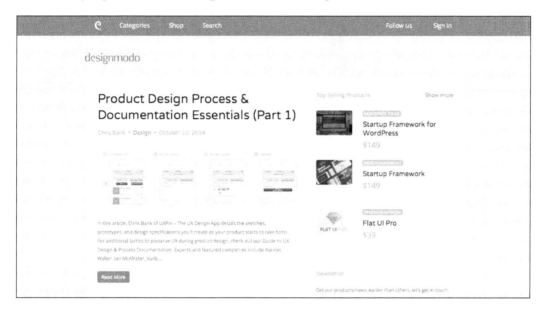

- **User interaction (desktop layout)**: The preceding screenshot shows the desktop version of a website that has a full menu, with functions such as **Sign In** and **Follow us** that are easy to access. The content is well spaced and feels clean. The column space on the right is used for calling action links that show some of their products. The column space on the left is reserved for more involving content, with images and headings.

Let's compare this to the mobile layout, which is shown in the following screenshot:

- **User interaction (mobile layout)**: In the mobile view, we can clearly see how the designers have made space for the content to take center stage on the site. The navigation collapses to show easily recognizable icons, and the main content takes up the rest of the page space, which is perfect for mobile phones.

- **Appearance** (focusing on content): When it comes to mobiles, content takes center stage. Studies indicate that some users leave a site after merely 3 seconds if the content has not loaded. Responsive web design puts the focus on content. When a mobile site loads, the content needs to be easy to find and should not force the user to scroll endlessly to find what they're looking for.

Management

Here are the benefits of responsive web design from the management perspective:

- **One code source**: Responsive websites have the advantage over the old mdot way of developing by virtue of keeping all of your code in one place. Another tremendous advantage of having one code source is that it avoids multiple redirects to an mdot web application. Redirects are very expensive in terms of load time and could add significant time to it.

- **Easier to maintain and update**: Besides one source code, the next obvious advantage is code that is easier to maintain. With all of the code centralized, it becomes a much less demanding task to keep all your sites up-to-date. One change on your desktop site will automatically reflect on both the tablet and mobile versions, without any extra development time.

The bad – slow load times and unresponsive interactions

Like most things, with the good comes the bad, and responsive web design is no different. Without proper optimization and careful planning, your responsive website could be slow and painful for the end user to navigate. Conscientious efforts to optimize the end user's experience are an integral part of good responsive design and development.

Slow load times

One of the biggest culprits when it comes to slow load times is images. All too often, the same-sized image used on the desktop site will be loaded for the mobile version as well. This is considered bad practice; when it comes to mobile browsing, every kilobyte counts. So, why let a user download a 300 kB file when they only need to download a 100 kB file? Creating appropriately sized images for various devices is a must.

Let's take a look at an example. The next two screenshots show a comparison of image downloads between desktop and mobile versions:

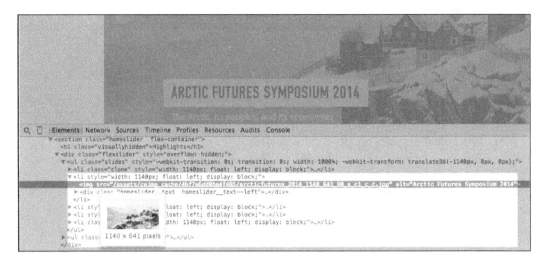

In the preceding screenshot, you can clearly see that the image downloaded is **1140** pixels wide by **641** pixels high. This is a fairly standard header image size for a desktop site to download. Now let's see what happens when the site is viewed at mobile size, as shown in the following screenshot:

In the mobile view, the website still looks great. The image is **385** pixels wide by **216** pixels high, but take note of the natural size of the image displayed. The natural size of the image is still **1140** pixels by **641** pixels. This means that the same image was downloaded to be displayed on the mobile website as the desktop layout. This might not seem like a big deal, but the experience of waiting to download an image of that size on a mobile device could very well lose you viewers on your website.

We will cover some great ways to avoid this problem a bit later. There are some excellent techniques available to manage your image downloading based on your current screen size.

Browser requests

Another cause of slow load times is the number of requests that your browser is making. Limiting the number of requests made to your server to download content, style sheets, or scripts will greatly improve your page's load times.

Using techniques such as **minification** to reduce the size of the response also goes a long way towards making your website load incredibly fast.

As an example, I've included the sizes of the two style sheets from the Bootstrap framework—bootstrap.css and boostrap.min.css. The latter is minified, and the former is not.

Take a look at the size difference between the two files, as shown here:

bootstrap.css	Stylesheet	304	Yes	129.44 KB
bootstrap.min.css	Stylesheet	304	Yes	106.95 KB

The file that has not been minified has added almost 24 kB to the request. That might not sound like a whole lot, but there are multiple requests for JavaScript files, cascading style sheets, and other scripts going on at the same time, and it'll all add up.

We will take a look at this a bit later, and discuss how to implement some simple code to reduce the number of requests made; we'll also explore which tools we can use to get our code *minified*.

Unresponsive interactions

Clicking on a button and not seeing an immediate response from a user interface can be terribly frustrating.

A website that is not optimized and downloads unnecessary JavaScript files and bloated HTML documents (among other things) is prone to performance issues when it comes to interaction with the server.

The ugly – the effects of slow performance

If you've ever opened a website and had to wait an inordinate amount of time for it to load, I don't have to tell you that it can become an annoyance. Not only do people disassociate from the brand, but they become frustrated and would rather try to find the content they want from a faster, more reliable source.

Effects on the end user

As mentioned before, we have mere seconds to engage the viewer.

Take this excerpt from a study done by KISSmetrics from the article, *How Loading Time Affects Your Bottom Line*, by *Sean Work*, as an indicator. For further information, please visit https://blog.kissmetrics.com/loading-time/

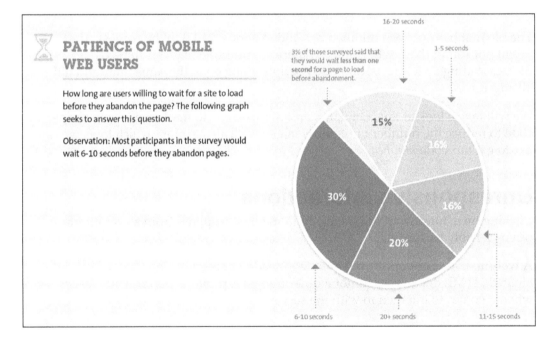

The preceding screenshots gives us some interesting facts:

- 73 percent of mobile Internet users say that they've encountered a website that was too slow upon loading

- 51 percent of mobile Internet users say that they've encountered a website that crashed, froze, or returned an error

- 38 percent of mobile Internet users say that they've encountered a website that wasn't available

- 47 percent of consumers expect a web page to load in 2 seconds or fewer

- 40 percent of people abandon a website that takes more than 3 seconds to load

- A 1-second delay in page response can result in a 7-percent reduction in conversions

- If an e-commerce site is making $100,000 per day, a 1-second page delay could potentially cost the company $2.5 million in lost sales every year

Effects on business

Improving a website could have a greater impact on your business than you may realize. This is a quote from an article at `http://www.getelastic.com/`:

> *"Walmart used a mix of pre-design, hands-on usability testing including paper-prototypes with post-design user tests (using moderated sessions throughout Canada) and on-site A/B testing, including an initial test of running both the responsive and non-responsive sites concurrently for about a week.*
>
> *Results were very positive for the responsive design. Conversion's up 20%, mobile orders up 98%."*
>
> *- Linda Bustos* (`http://www.getelastic.com/how-walmart-cas-responsive-redesign-boost-conversion-by-20/`)

Let's take a look at this simple but informative image detailing the effects that load times have on consumers. It's clear that slow load times have a tremendously negative effect on consumers who shop online:

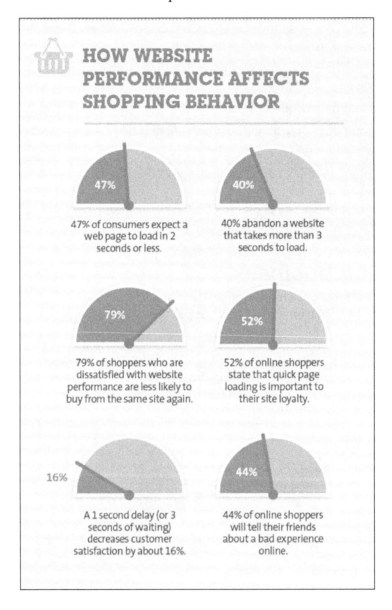

Summary

In this chapter, we covered briefly what responsive design is, and more importantly, why it's so important in today's webscape.

Responsive web design helps us create a more uniform appearance across an array of devices, and leaves users feeling more familiar with a brand, regardless of the device they're using to interact with it.

Code is kept together in one place and negates the need to maintain multiple pages or documents for one website.

Code that has not been optimized and reckless content download can cause websites that look great to feel terrible. This could potentiality cause users to leave the site before it's even done loading. In some cases, it may even cost you money. With all of that out of the way, let's get practical and start improving our responsive website's performance. We'll look at the placement of our resources, how to avoid common mistakes with `<image>` tags, and some other great techniques that we can apply instantly to see an improvement in website load times.

2

Tweaking Your Website for Performance

Right, you must be tired of reading! Well, you'll be happy to know that, from here on, things get a lot more hands-on. In this chapter, we will look at some basic techniques that are available to improve the loading of your website, such as the correct placement of **Document Object Model** (**DOM**) elements, and some more advanced techniques such as preloading your content.

But before we get there, let's start with something simple.

Resource placement on the DOM

When you develop a website, it's easy to forget that the placement of elements in the DOM can make a difference to the time it takes to load the content the user views on the site.

Now that we throw all kinds of wonderful scripts into our websites to create mesmerizing animations and make our site responsive, the placement of resources in our DOM is even more relevant.

Yahoo! released a tool (YSlow) a couple of years ago that measured a website's performance, showing what loads and when. With that information, it gave people recommendations to improve the site's performance. One of these recommendations is to put the `<script>` tags at the bottom of the page just before the closing `</body>` tag.

Let's now take a look at the following code snippet and understand it:

```
<head>
<!-- Styles -->
<link rel="stylesheet" href="css/style.css" type="text/css" />
<!-- Scripts -->
<script src="//ajax.googleapis.com/ajax/libs/jquery/1.11.1/jquery.min.
js"
type="text/javascript" language="Javascript"></script>
</head>
```

Technically, there is nothing wrong with this. The tags have all the needed attributes, the types have been defined correctly, and both resources point to a valid file.

Making a simple change to this code can speed up the page load of your website. So, what's the change?

First, remove the script from the `<head>` tag, like this:

```
<head>
<link rel="stylesheet" href="css/style.css" type="text/css" />
</head>
```

Then place this exact JavaScript code just before the `<body>` closing tag, as follows:

```
<body>
<script src="//ajax.googleapis.com/ajax/libs/jquery/1.11.1/jquery.min.
js"
type="text/javascript" language="Javascript"></script>
</body>
```

That simple? Yes, it is.

You might ask why this improves the page load, and should you always do this, for every `<script>` tag? Let's talk about it. The reason for the improved page load time is simple. When the server is busy sending the resources placed in the `<head>` tag, the browser starts to download the files, `query.min.js` in this case.

Downloading the example code

You can download the example code files for all Packt books you have purchased from your account at http://www.packtpub.com. If you purchased this book elsewhere, you can visit http://www.packtpub.com/support and register to have the files e-mailed directly to you.

Most browsers download JavaScript synchronously. So, none of your markup or images will load while the JavaScript is downloading from the server. Hence, it slows down the page load time. Visually, the DOM doesn't start to *render* until the files are completely downloaded and the user is faced with an empty website, just waiting for your beautiful design to come into view. When scripts prevent the page from loading, we refer to it as **render blocking**.

On the other hand, if you place your JavaScript resources at the bottom of the page, immediately before the closing `</body>` tag, the page will render the markup, load the images, and then load the JavaScript in the background. Let's take a look at this representation for some more clarity:

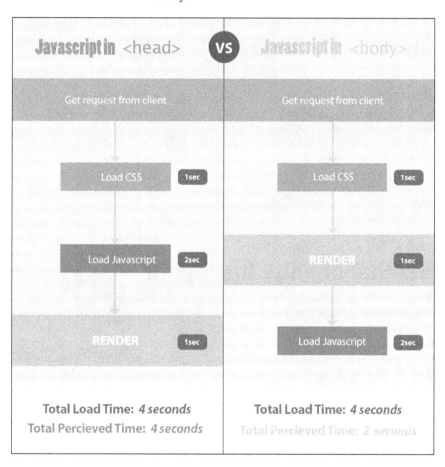

In the preceding diagram, you can clearly see that the user will perceive the site with the script in the <head> as loading more slowly than the site with the script in the <body> tag. In reality, the sites had the same load time. With the advantage of faster load time, you might be faced with some interactivity on the website if JavaScript is required to trigger certain UI events.

 There has always been much debate whether this should always be done. There are definite advantages when placing <script> tags at the end of the page. Like everything, there are two sides to an argument. Generally, each project you do will have different requirements, and this will need to be tailored to suit the project you are working on.

Scripts with $(document).ready()

If you use jQuery, then you most certainly make use of the $(document).ready() code block.

What this does is that it starts to execute the code only after the DOM has been loaded. Therefore, you can place the scripts using the $(document).ready handler at the bottom of the <body> tag:

```
$(document).ready(function(){
    // The DOM is now loaded and the handler for .ready() has been
    // called.
});
```

Scripts that change the layout

Often in responsive websites, we use scripts to modify the layout of the page, depending on what device it is being viewed on, the current size of the browser window, or even what capabilities the device has.

In cases like these, it is often preferred to load those scripts first. When the DOM is ready to be rendered, the scripts are ready to perform the adjustments to the HTML, and do not leave the user viewing a mangled site.

If you use jQuery for the layout script, there is a trade-off to be made. You'll have to load jQuery in the `<head>` tag before you include the layout script. Let's work through this example together.

First, let's just understand what our goal is. We want to develop a site that looks good when the user sees it for the first time and loads as fast as possible.

The welcome section

Here is a screenshot that shows the **welcome** section, which is just a simple landing page with a wide header and some body text:

The information section

The following screenshot shows the next section, the **info** section, which is the same as the first section but with a different background color:

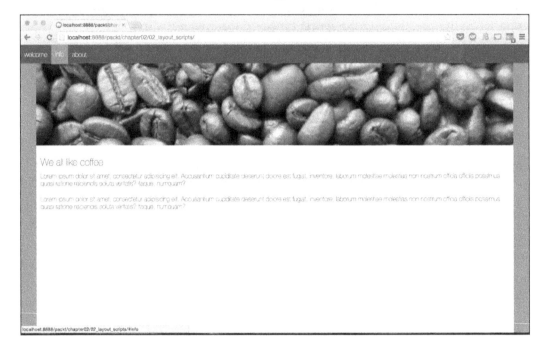

The about section

The following is a screenshot of the **about** section:

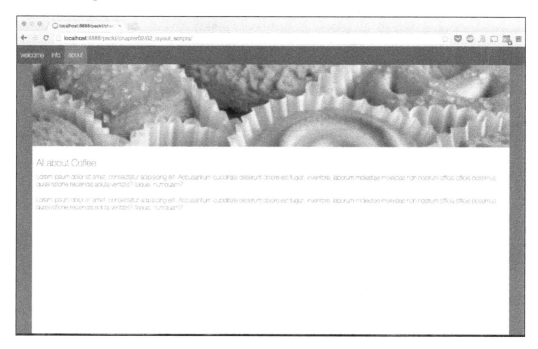

The first thing we need to do is use some jQuery to make the sections fit into the viewport. Then we'll look at ways to improve the site further.

Alright, now that you have the project open in your favorite editor, let's start improving this site.

Adjusting the sections

Let's now tweak the settings:

1. Open the `layout.js` file from the **js** folder, as shown in the following screenshot:

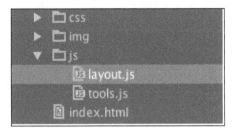

2. You should see the following code:

```
1  jQuery(document).ready(function($){
2      // cache the window object
3      var win = $(window);
4      // adjust the section to fit the size of the viewport.
5  });
6
```

3. Below the comment (denoted by //), adjust the section. On line **5**, add the following code to let the sections fit into the viewport:

```
$('.full-h').css({
    height: win.height()
});
```

4. Refresh the site in your browser, and you should now see that the sections fit into the document window, as shown in the following screenshot:

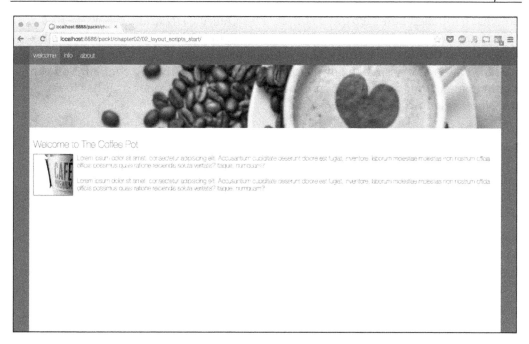

Even though the site loads perfectly well and the sections fit well into the viewport, just as the site loads you see the sections on the page for a brief moment, as shown in the following screenshot:

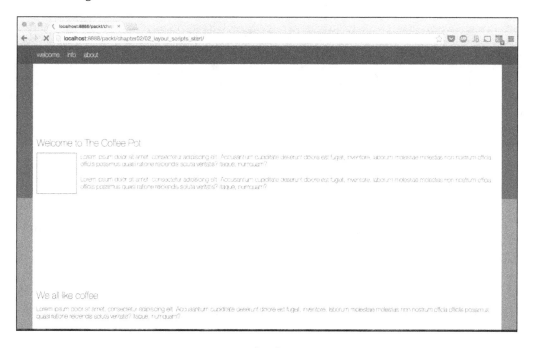

So what happened here? It's quite simple. The jQuery CDN and `layout.js` files are placed just before the closing `</body>` tag. While the DOM is being rendered, the JavaScript is still downloading and executes a brief moment after the DOM has been parsed. This is a very small example of a project with hardly any content. You can just imagine having a wealth of content loading while your poor user has to see your site all mangled up.

Improving the output

The first thing we do is move the scripts from the bottom, up to the `<head>` tags. Now remember, if you use jQuery to handle the layout, as we do in this example, you need to move jQuery to the `<head>` as well.

Ideally, using plain JavaScript would be a much faster solution. So, if it's possible, consider using a pure JavaScript solution to further improve the speed of the site. It might take a bit longer to script, but we are going for performance here, aren't we? This is illustrated in the following steps:

1. Open the `index.html` file and go to lines **81** and **82**:

```
80    <!-- Javascript -->
81    <script type="text/javascript" src="//code.jquery.com/jquery-1.11.1.min.js"></script>
82    <script type="text/javascript" src="js/layout.js"></script>
```

2. Let's simply move those two lines (**81** and **82**) into the `<head>` tags:

```
3     <head lang="en">
4         <meta charset="UTF-8">
5         <title></title>
6         <!-- Stylesheets -->
7         <link rel="stylesheet" type="text/css" href="css/style.css" />
8         <!-- Layout Javascript -->
9         <script type="text/javascript" src="//code.jquery.com/jquery-1.11.1.min.js"></script>
10        <script type="text/javascript" src="js/layout.js"></script>
11    </head>
```

3. Place the code immediately after the `<link/>` tag for the style sheet. Refresh the site, and voilà! Your user might wait a tiny bit longer but, when the site displays, it's as you intended it to look.

4. Often, after fixing one problem, another pops up. In this case, the user will have to wait a bit longer while the JavaScript in the `<head>` tag loads. Here is a simple way to make the user's wait a bit less painful.

5. In the `index.html` file, navigate to the first line after the opening `<body>` tag. Once there, place the following code:

```
<div class="loader">
    <div class="spinner">Loading...</div>
</div>
```

6. Okay, simple three lines! Here's what we intend to do with them: display a loader while the user waits for our site to load. Once the site has been loaded, we will simply remove the loader from the DOM.

7. Open the `style.css` file in the `css` folder. Underneath the code for the `nav`, item place the following CSS code:

```
loader {
    position: absolute;
    top: 0;
    left: 0;
    z-index: 10;
    background: rgba(0,0,0,0.9);
    width: 100%;
    height: 100%;
}
.progress_bar {
    text-align: center;
    padding-top: 20px;
    color: #FFF;
    width: 200px;
    height: 20px;
    margin-top: 45px;
    background: url("../img/spinner.gif") no-repeat;
    background-size: 200px 20px;
}
```

This will create a 90-percent opaque layer that stretches over the entire view, and will place a loader centered on the screen that informs the user that something is happening.

Your result should look like this:

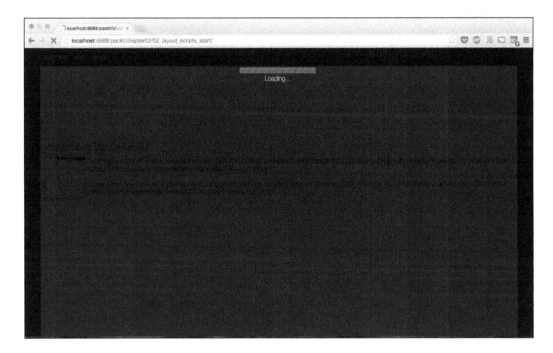

I've always been a firm believer in *"Don't reinvent the wheel."* With that in mind, this next bit talks about a jQuery plugin developed by an exciting group at **CreateJS** that assists you in preloading content on your website.

What does CreateJS do for us? CreateJS is a JavaScript library that allows us to easily set up preloading and perform complex animations, among other things.

You can head over to `http://www.createjs.com/Downloads` and copy the CDN path from the middle of that page. At the time of writing this book, the version of CreateJS is 0.4.1, as shown in the following screenshot:

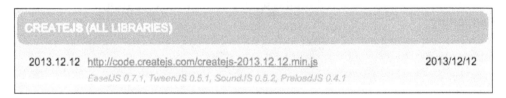

Supported file types for the `LoadQueue` function are as follows:

- **BINARY**: Raw binary data via XHR
- **CSS**: CSS files
- **IMAGE**: Common image formats
- **JAVASCRIPT**: JavaScript files
- **JSON**: JSON data
- **JSONP**: Cross-domain JSON files
- **MANIFEST**: A list of files to load in JSON format
- **SOUND**: Audio file formats
- **SVG**: SVG Files
- **XML**: XML Data

It's time to do some coding.

We're going to add a gallery section and use `preloadjs` to load the images for the gallery. In addition to loading the gallery, we will bind event listeners for progress, a single item completed, all items completed, and when an error occurs:

1. Let's start by adding the link to the `nav` item:

```
<li id="anchor-gallery">
    <a class="anchor" href="#gallery">gallery</a>
</li>
```

2. This will add a new `nav` item labeled `gallery`. Now we are going to make a section for this `nav` item to scroll to:

```
<section id="gallery" class="full-h">
    <div class="container">
        <div class="img-wrapper">
            <img src="http://mrg.bz/POKzTi" alt=""/>
        </div>
        <div class="content">
            <h2>Gallery</h2>
            <div class="gallery-container">
                <div class="gallery-wrapper">
                </div>
            </div>
        </div>
    </div>
</section>
```

This provides us with a `<div>` tag for the preloader to append the images to. The `<div>` tag we will use for this is `gallery-wrapper`.

Let's move on to instantiating `createjs` and adding the functions we'll use to handle the loading.

Add the following code immediately before the closing `<body>` tag, including the `createjs` library:

```
<script type="text/javascript"
src="http://code.createjs.com/createjs-
2013.12.12.min.js"></script>
```

3. Instantiate `createjs` and create an array of images to load:

```
var queue = new createjs.LoadQueue(false);
// Images to load
var images = [
    {id: "001", src: "img/001.jpg"},
    {id: "002", src: "img/002.jpg"},
    {id: "003", src: "img/003.jpg"},
    {id: "004", src: "img/004.jpg"},
    {id: "005", src: "img/005.jpg"},
    {id: "006", src: "img/006.jpg"},
    {id: "007", src: "img/007.jpg"},
    {id: "008", src: "img/008.jpg"},
    {id: "009", src: "img/009.jpg"},
    {id: "0010", src: "img/010.jpg"},
    {id: "0011", src: "img/011.jpg"}
];
```

4. Let's create the functions that bind to the different events:

```
// Event listener for when file is uploaded
function hndlUpload(event)
{
    console.log('File '+event.item.id+' loaded:
'+event.item.type);
}
// EventListener to track upload progress
function hndlProgress(event)
{
```

```
        console.log('File loading: '+ (queue.progress*100|0) +
" % Loaded");
}
// EventListener when error occurred
function loadError(event)
{
        console.log("An Error occurred: "+ event.text);
}
// When All files have loaded
function loadComplete(event)
{
        var $gallery_wrapper = $('.gallery-wrapper');
        for (var i  = 0; i < images.length; i++)
{
            var img = queue.getResult(images[i].id);
            var img_wrapper = '<div class="gallery-img"><img
src="'+img.src+'" /></div>';
            $gallery_wrapper.append(img_wrapper);
        }
        $gallery_wrapper.append('<div class="clear-
left"></div>');
}
```

5. Now that we've created the functions— event handlers, in this case—we need to add the event listeners:

```
// Add event listeners
queue.addEventListener('complete', loadComplete);
queue.addEventListener("fileload", hndlUpload);
queue.addEventListener("progress", hndlProgress);
queue.addEventListener("error", loadError);
queue.loadManifest(images);
```

Great! That covers the code. Now let's take a look at the result and talk about what we did:

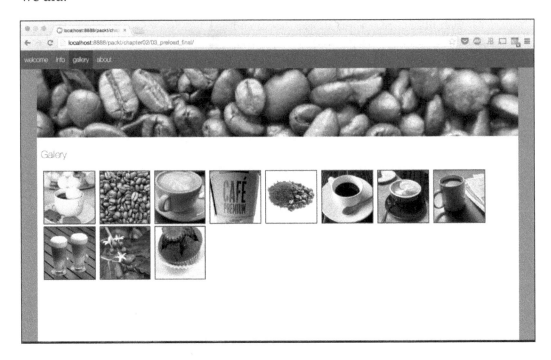

In the preceding screenshot, you can see that the gallery wrapper has been populated with the images from our image array. The advantage of this is that the DOM can render while the JavaScript is loading the images and appending them to the gallery wrapper.

Adding a simple GIF loading icon in the gallery section might be useful if you have a large number of images or, even better, make use of lazy loading to load images.

If you look in the **Console** section of your browser you can see the output of the JavaScript code. Here is a screenshot of the example code's output:

```
Q  🔍    Elements  Network  Sources  Timeline  Profiles  Resources  Audits  Console
🚫  ▽   <top frame>                    ▼   Preserve log
🔟 File loading: 0 % Loaded
   File loading: 9 % Loaded
   File 001 loaded: image
   File loading: 18 % Loaded
   File 002 loaded: image
   File loading: 27 % Loaded
   File 003 loaded: image
   File loading: 36 % Loaded
   File 004 loaded: image
   File loading: 45 % Loaded
   File 005 loaded: image
   File loading: 54 % Loaded
```

You can see information about the image being loaded, how far it is from finishing, and when it finishes loading. This code can be adapted to create informative loading screens when you have a large gallery or data file that needs to load.

There are also other solutions worth taking a look at that are not jQuery-dependent, including RequireJS.

DNS prefetching

DNS prefetching is a useful technique when your website accesses multiple sites that are on different domains.

Here is a code snippet of a DNS prefetch that is placed in the `<head>` tags:

```
<link rel="dns-prefetch" href="http://www.paperjetwednesday.com/">
```

The purpose of DNS prefetching

DNS prefetching attempts to resolve the domain names before the user follows a link to that domain. If the domain has been resolved, the advantage of this will be that there is effectively no delay due to DNS name resolution.

An excellent example of using DNS prefetching would be for results in a search that link to various other domains. Here are a few types of prefetching:

- -prefetch: This identifies a resource file, such as an image or a CSS style sheet, to be included in the cache

- -dns-prefetch: This identifies a DNS query to resolve the background so that requests can occur more quickly

- -prerender (IE only): This identifies a web page to load in the background, if the user wants to navigate to it next

Too many DOM Elements

Another big problem with responsive design is hiding and revealing elements based on the current viewport resolution.

Often, the `display: none` CSS attribute is used to hide the element. It has the effect that you'd expect—it hides the element from the DOM. Being hidden doesn't mean that it's not being rendered in the background.

Hiding an image, for instance, will still make an HTTP request, adding to the load time of your website. Ways to work around this will be discussed in more detail in the next chapter.

Summary

Right, that was quite a mouthful! We looked at quite a few things in this chapter.

The importance of resource placement on the DOM is often overlooked. It's true that placing scripts at the bottom of the page certainly improves performance, but it's also true that some scripts do need to load before the DOM renders (in the case of our example, to adjust the layout).

Using the technique of preloading content can be greatly helpful in improving the initial load of your site. The example showed a gallery that did not exist in the initial DOM render, but the preloaded images were appended into a gallery wrapper once they had been loaded. The great thing about this is that you can create informative feedback using a plugin such as `createjs`.

DNS prefetching is a very helpful piece of code that can resolve the DNS name in the background for the site that your page might point to. Search engines can greatly benefit from this.

Showing and hiding elements might seem like a great idea, but there are times when a better solution exists. A hidden image will still prompt an HTTP response and slow down the load of your DOM. We'll talk about some excellent techniques in the next chapter to improve on this.

3
Managing Images

Cats, dogs and all sorts of memes, the Internet as we know it today is dominated by images. You can open almost any web page and you'll surely find images on the page.

The more interactive our web browsing experience becomes, the more images we tend to use. So, it is tremendously important to ensure that the images we use are optimized and loaded as fast as possible. We should also make sure that we choose the correct image type.

In this chapter we will talk about, why image formats are important, conditional loading, visibility for DOM elements, specifying sizes, media queries, introducing sprite sheets, and caching.

Let's talk basics.

Choosing the correct image format

Deciding what image format to use is usually the first step you take when you start your website. Take a look at this table for an overview and comparison of the available image formats:

Format	Features
GIF	256 colors
	Support for animation
	Transparency
PNG	256 colors
	True colors
	Transparency

Format	Features
JPEG/JPG	256 colors
	True colors

From the preceding listed formats, you can conclude that, if you had a complex image that was 1000 x 1000 pixels, the image in the JPEG format would be the smallest in file size. This also means that it would load the fastest.

The smallest image is not always the best choice though. If you need to have images with transparent parts, you'll have to use the PNG or GIF formats and if you need an animation, you are stuck with using a GIF format or the lesser know APNG format.

Optimizing images

Optimizing your image can have a huge impact on your overall website performance.

There are some great applications to help you with image optimization and compression. TinyPNG is a great example of a site that helps you to compress you PNG's images online for free. They also have a Photoshop plugin that is available for download at `https://tinypng.com/`.

Another great application to help you with JPG compression is JPEGMini. Head over to `http://www.jpegmini.com/` to get a copy for either Windows or Mac OS X.

Another application that is worth considering is **Radical Image Optimization Tool (RIOT)**. It is a free program and can be found at `http://luci.criosweb.ro/riot/`. RIOT is a Windows application.

Viewing as JPEG is not the only image format that we use in the Web; you can also look at a Mac OS X application called ImageOptim (`http://www.imageoptim.com`) It is also a free application and compresses both JPEG and PNG images.

If you are not on Mac OS X, you can head over to `https://tinypng.com/`. This handy little site allows you to upload your image to the site, where it is then compressed. The optimized images are then linked to the site as downloadable files.

As JPEG image formats make up the majority of most web pages, with some exceptions, lets take a look at how to make your images load faster.

Progressive images

Most advanced image editors such as Photoshop and GIMP give you the option to encode your JPEG images using either baseline or progressive.

If you **Save For Web** using Photoshop, you will see this section at the top of the dialog box:

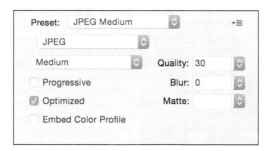

In most cases, for use on web pages, I would advise you to use the **Progressive** encoding type. When you save an image using baseline, the full image data of every pixel block is written to the file one after the other. Baseline images load gradually from the top-left corner.

If you save an image using the **Progressive** option, then it saves only a part of each of these blocks to the file and then another part and so on, until the entire image's information is captured in the file. When you render a progressive image, you will see a very grainy image display and this will gradually become sharper as it loads. Progressive images are also smaller than baseline images for various technical reasons. This means that they load faster. In addition, they appear to load faster when something is displayed on the screen.

Here is a typical example of the visual difference between loading a progressive and a baseline JPEG image:

Here, you can clearly see how the two encodings load in a browser. On the left, the progressive image is already displayed whereas the baseline image is still loading from the top.

Alright, that was some really basic stuff, but it was extremely important nonetheless. Let's move on to conditional loading.

Adaptive images

Adaptive images are an adaptation of Filament Group's context-aware image sizing experiment.

What does it do? Well, this is what the guys say about themselves:

> "**Adaptive images** *detects your visitor's screen size and automatically creates, caches, and delivers device appropriate re-scaled versions of your web page's embedded HTML images. No mark-up changes needed. It is intended for use with Responsive Designs and to be combined with Fluid Images techniques.*"

It certainly trumps the experiment in the simplicity of implementation.

So, how does it work?

It's quite simple. There is no need to change any of your current code. Head over to http://adaptive-images.com/download.htm and get the latest version of adaptive images.

You can place the adaptive-images.php file in the root of your site. Make sure to add the content of the .htaccess file to your own as well. Head over to the index file of your site and add this in the <head> tags:

```
<script>document.cookie='resolution='+Math.max(screen.width,screen.
height)+'; path=/';</script>
```

Note that it is has to be in the <head> tag of your site.

Open the adaptive-images.php file and add you media query values into the $resolutions variable.

Here is a snippet of code that is pretty self-explanatory:

```
$resolutions    = array(1382, 992, 768, 480);
$cache_path     = "ai-cache";
$jpg_quality    = 80;
$sharpen        = TRUE;
$watch_cache    = TRUE;
$browser_cache = 60*60*24*7;
```

The $resolution variable accepts the break-points that you use for your website. You can simply add the value of the screen width in pixels. So, in the the preceding example, it would read 1382 pixels as the first break-point, 992 pixels as the second one, and so on.

The cache path tells adaptive images where to store the generated resized images. It's a relative path from your document root. So, in this case, your folder structure would read as document_root/a-cache/{images stored here}.

The next variable, $jpg_quality, sets the quality of any generated JPGs images on a scale of 0 to 100.

Shrinking images could cause blurred details. Set $sharpen to TRUE to perform a sharpening process on rescaled images.

When you set `$watch_cache` to TRUE, you force adaptive images to check that the adapted image isn't stale; that is, it ensures that the updated source images are recached.

Lastly, `$browser_cache` sets how long the browser cache should last for. The values are seconds, minutes, hours, days (7 days by default). You can change the last digit to modify the days. So, if you want images to be cached for two days, simply change the last value to 2.

Then,… oh wait, that's all? It is indeed!

Adaptive images will work with your existing website and they don't require any markup changes. They are also device-agnostic and follow a mobile-first philosophy.

Conditional loading

Responsive designs combine three main techniques, which are as follows:

- Fluid grids
- Flexible images
- Media queries

The technique that I want to focus on in this section is *media queries*. In most cases, developers use media queries to change the layout, width height, padding, font size and so on, depending on conditions related to the viewport.

Let's see how we can achieve conditional image loading using CSS3's image-set function:

```
.my-background-img {
background-image: image-set(
 url(icon1x.jpg) 1x,
 url(icon2x.jpg) 2x
);
}
```

You can see in the preceding piece of CSS3 code that the image is loaded conditionally based on its display type. The second statement `url(icon2x.jpg)  2x` would load the hi-resolution image or retina image. This reduces the number of CSS rules we have to create. Maintaining a site with a lot of background images can become quite a chore if a separate rule exists for each one.

Here is a simple media query example:

```
@media screen and (max-width: 480px) {
    .container {
        width: 320px;
    }
}
```

As I'm sure you already know, this snippet tells the browser that, for any device with a viewport of fewer than 480 pixels, any element with the class container has to be 320 pixels wide.

 When you use media queries, always make sure to include the viewport <meta> tag in the head of your HTML document, as follows:
```
<meta name="viewport" content="width=device-width,
initial-scale=1">
```

I've included this template here as I'd like to start with this. It really makes it very easy to get started with new responsive projects:

```
/* MOBILE */
@media screen and (max-width: 480px) {
    .container {
        width: 320px;
    }
}
/* TABLETS */
@media screen and (min-width: 481px) and (max-width: 720px) {
    .container {
        width: 480px;
    }
}
/* SMALL DESKTOP OR LARGE TABLETS */
@media screen and (min-width: 721px) and (max-width: 960px) {
    .container {
        width: 720px;
    }
}
/* STANDARD DESKTOP */
@media screen and (min-width: 961px) and (max-width: 1200px) {
    .container {
        width: 960px;
    }
}
```

```
/* LARGE DESKTOP */
@media screen and (min-width: 1201px) and (max-width: 1600px) {
    .container {
        width: 1200px;
    }
}
/* EXTRA LARGE DESKTOP */
@media screen and (min-width: 1601px) {
    .container {
        width: 1600px;
    }
}
```

When you view a website on a desktop, it's quite a common thing to have a left and a right column. Generally, the left column contains information that requires more focus and the right column contains content with a bit less importance. In some cases, you might even have three columns. Take the social website Facebook as an example.

At the time of writing this book, Facebook used a three-column layout, which is as follows:

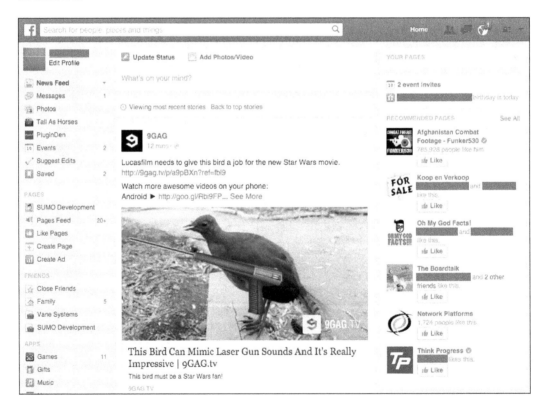

When you view a web page on a mobile device, you won't be able to fit all three columns into the smaller viewport. So, you'd probably want to hide some of the columns and not request the data that is usually displayed in the columns that are hidden.

Alright, we've done some talking. Well, you've done some reading. Now, let's get into our code!

Our goal in this section is to learn about conditional development, with the focus on images. I've constructed a little website with a two-column layout. The left column houses the content and the right column is used to populate a little news feed. I made a simple PHP script that returns a JSON object with the news items.

Here is a preview of the different screens that we will work on:

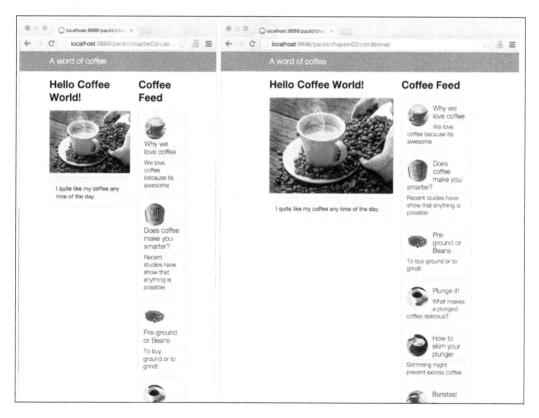

These two views are a result of the queries that are shown in the following style sheet code:

```
/* MOBILE */
@media screen and (max-width: 480px) {
}
/* TABLETS */
@media screen and (min-width: 481px) and (max-width: 720px) {
}
```

Here is a another preview:

These two views are a result of the queries that shown in the following style sheet code:

```
/* SMALL DESKTOP OR LARGE TABLETS */
@media screen and (min-width: 721px) and (max-width: 960px) {

}
/* STANDARD DESKTOP */
@media screen and (min-width: 961px) and (max-width: 1200px) {
}
```

This is another screenshot example:

Lastly, these two views will be a result of the remaining queries that are shown in the following style sheet code:

```
/* LARGE DESKTOP */
@media screen and (min-width: 1201px) and (max-width: 1600px) {
}
/* EXTRA LARGE DESKTOP */
@media screen and (min-width: 1601px) { }
```

We'll discuss media queries in more detail in the next section.

Let's start coding our conditional loading column.

Open the `index.html` file and add the following code inside the `<div class="left"></div>` tag:

```
<div class="content">
    <h2>Hello Coffee World!</h2>
    <div class="content-body">
        <img src="img/progressive.jpg" alt="Coffee" />
        <div class="box">
            <small>I quite like my coffee any time of the
day.</small>
        </div>
    </div>
</div>
```

Just below this, also in the `index.html` page, add the following code in the `<div class="right"></div>` tag:

```
<h2>Coffee Feed</h2>
<div class="news">
</div>
```

This is simple enough, right? The best way to load the news when using conditional loading is usually with some sort of web service. In this example, we'll just make use of a simple jQuery GET function. The function will make a get request to a PHP file called `news.php`. The function inside this file is called `getNews`. This will return a JSON object to our JavaScript, which we can then start using to manipulate the DOM while still allowing our web page to load in the background.

Here is the JavaScript code that will just check whether the screen size is appropriate to load the content. Add it at the bottom of the page, just before the `<body>` tag of the document in the `index.html` file, as shown in the following code snippet:

```
<script src="//ajax.googleapis.com/ajax/libs/jquery/1.11.1/jquery.min.
js">
</script>
<script type="text/javascript" language="JavaScript">
$(document).ready(function(){ // ready handler
    if ($(window).width() > 720) {
// GET Request to news source.
        $.ajax({
            url: 'news.php',
            beforeSend: function() {
                // Display loader in the news column
                $('.spinner').css({
                    display: 'inline-block'
                });
            },
            type: 'GET',
            dataType: 'json',
            data: {
                func: 'getNews'
            }
        }).done(function(data){
            // Success
            var item = '';
            for (var i = 0; i < data.length;i++) {
                item += '<div class="news-item">';
                item += '<img src="'+data[i].images['thumb']+'"
/>';
                item += '<h4>'+data[i].title+'</h4><hr />';
                item += '<p>'+data[i].intro+'</p>';
                item += '</div>';
                $('.news').append(item);
                item = '';
            }
        }).fail(function(){
            // Failed
            $('.news').append('<p>Could not connect to the news
source.</p>');
        }).always(function(){
            // Always run this code
```

```
        // Remove spinner
        $('.spinner').remove();
      });
  } else {
      $('.right').remove();
      $('.left').addClass('col-full');
  }
});
</script>
```

Let's take a look at the JavaScript code and break it down to see what it does:

```
if ($(window).width() > 720) {
```

As the name suggests, conditional loading occurs if certain conditions are met. In the case of this example, if the screen size is greater than 720 pixels, the right-hand column will be loaded with the news feed.

This is not all. Besides the news items being added only when the screen size is greater than 720 pixels, the important part of this code is that the **Asynchronous Javascript And XML (AJAX)** call will be made only if the condition is met. AJAX calls can be quite strenuous on the browser if they are not controlled.

Another important part of this is that the right-hand column is not simply hidden if the device viewport is smaller than 720 pixels; it is removed from the DOM, which brings me to my next point. There are too many DOM elements lying dormant in a lot of websites.

One-to-many DOM elements

I briefly touched on this subject in the previous chapter, so let's talk about this a bit more. A great article about showing and hiding elements by Josh Powell can be found at `http://www.learningjquery.com/2010/05/now-you-see-me-showhide-performance/`.

He compared the speed of showing and hiding elements using different techniques and found that the enabling and disabling of style sheets is the fastest method to show and hide elements on your page. Now, for responsive design, this is very handy, but I feel that hiding elements is being used rather carelessly. When an element is hidden from the viewport of your browser, it still renders when the page is loaded. If you have a lot of elements, they'll all have to render before the page has finished loading. Even worse, if you have images in the section that you are hiding, those requests are still being made to the server.

I propose a better solution. Create a simple rendering function or two rendering functions that can recreate certain sections in your page, rather than simply showing and hiding elements. This way, unnecessary requests will be eliminated and your user will still be able to enjoy a fast-loading page. Why don't we try to make a simple function to do that for us? In the project, you should have a index file, an empty `render.js` file, and a style sheet called `styles.css`. All the styles have already been done, so we just need to fill in the JavaScript part.

Open the `render.js` file and let's get cracking!

We will use an anonymous function to make our render engine example. The methods that we will create are as follows:

- `init`
- `addGallery`
- `removeGallery`
- `getGalleryImages`
- `showImage`
- `removeModal`

Lets start the script and create the `init` method:

```
(function(window, $) {
window.renderEngine = {
init: function() {
    if ($(window).width() > 720) {
        this.addGallery();
    } else {
        this.removeGallery();
    }

    $('.gallery-img').bind('click', function() {
        renderEngine.showImage($(this));
    });
},
// Next method comes here
};
})(window, jQuery);
```

Similar to the previous example, we'll use `720` pixels as the break-point. The `init` method will load when the document is ready. If the window's width is greater than `720` pixels, we will create the gallery section in the document. If the window's width is fewer than `720` pixels, we will not create the section and will avoid excess DOM elements.

Let's move on. Directly after the `init` method, we will create the `addGallery` method. To do this, add the following code after the closing bracket of the `init` method:

```
addGallery: function() {
    var gallery = '<div id="gallery"><h4>Click on an image to
create a modal</h4><ul>';
    var images = this.getGalleryImages();
    console.log(images.length);
    for (var i = 0; i < images.length;i++)
    {
        gallery += '<li><img class="gallery-img"
src="'+images[i].thumb_src+'" title="'+images[i].title+'"
width="100" data-src="'+images[i].src+'" /></li>';
    }
    gallery += '</ul></div>';
    $('#gallery-container').append(gallery);
},
```

This method makes a call to another function in the object called `getGalleryImages()`. Now, this function could contain an AJAX call or another type of web service that returns an array of image information to you. For this example, however, we will simply return an array of objects.

The function creates a list of images in the container called `gallery`. It also creates a `data-src` attribute that we'll use a bit later. Now the `removeGallery` function comes next:

```
removeGallery: function () {
    if ($('#gallery').length) {
        $('#gallery').remove();
    }
    $('body').append('<p>Hey! Who needs a gallery!</p>');
},
```

This is nice and simple, right? All this does is check whether or not the gallery element has been created; if it has been created, it completely removes it from the DOM and appends a cheeky message to it instead. Here is the `getGalleryImages` function that returns an array of image objects:

```
getGalleryImages: function() {
    return [
        {
            src: 'img/001.jpg',
            thumb_src: 'img/thumbs/001.jpg',
            title: 'One'
        },
        {
            src: 'img/002.jpg',
            thumb_src: 'img/thumbs/002.jpg',
            title: 'Two'
        },
        {
            src: 'img/003.jpg',
            thumb_src: 'img/thumbs/003.jpg',
            title: 'Three'
        },
        {
            src: 'img/004.jpg',
            thumb_src: 'img/thumbs/004.jpg',
            title: 'Four'
        }
    ];
},
```

Nothing much to be said here. This simply returns an array of image objects with three properties, `src`, `thumb_src`, and `title`.

Now comes the beefy method. This dynamically creates a `modal` window with an overlay, as shown in the following code snippet:

```
showImage: function($image) {
    var height = $(window).height() * 0.8;
    var width = $(window).width() * 0.8;
    var left = ($(window).width() / 2) - width / 2;
```

```
        var top = ($(window).height() / 2) - height / 2;
        var imgHeight = height * 0.8;
        var modalStyle = 'style="width: '+width+'px; height:'+height+'px;
    left: '+left+'px; top: '+top+'px;"';

        var modal = '<div id="gallery-modal" class="modal">';
        modal += '<div class="overlay"></div>';
        modal += '<div class="modal-body" '+modalStyle+'>';
        modal += '<div class="modal-close" onclick="renderEngine.
    removeModal()">X</div>';
        modal += '<h2>'+$image.attr('title')+'</h2><hr />';
        modal += '<img src="'+$image.attr('data-src')+'"
    height="'+imgHeight+'" style="height:'+imgHeight+'px;
    width:'+imgHeight+'px;"/>';
        modal += '</div>';
        modal += '</div>';
        $('body').append(modal);
    },
```

This is a very manual method but, for the purposes of this demo, it'll do just fine.

The last method removes the modal window, as shown in the following code snippet:

```
removeModal: function() {
    var modal = document.getElementById('gallery-modal');
    $(modal).fadeOut(600);
    setTimeout(function(){
        $('.modal').remove();
    },700);
}
```

This is also nice and simple. It hides the modal window and completely removes it from the DOM after 700 ms because there's no need for the modal window to be there if it's not going to be used.

Here is the final complete code for the renderEngine demo:

```
(function(window, $) {
    window.renderEngine = {
        init: function() {
        },
        addGallery: function() {
            var gallery = '<div id="gallery"><h4>Click on an image
    to create a modal</h4><ul>';
```

```
        var images = this.getGalleryImages();
        console.log(images.length);
        for (var i = 0; i < images.length;i++)
        {
            gallery += '<li><img class="gallery-img"
src="'+images[i].thumb_src+'" title="'+images[i].title+'"
width="100" data-src="'+images[i].src+'" /></li>';
        }
        gallery += '</ul></div>';
        $('#gallery-container').append(gallery);
    },
    removeGallery: function () {
        if ($('#gallery').length) {
            $('#gallery').remove();
        }
        $('body').append('<p>Hey! Who needs a gallery!</p>');
    },
    getGalleryImages: function() {
        return [
            {
                src: 'img/001.jpg',
                thumb_src: 'img/thumbs/001.jpg',
                title: 'One'
            },
            {
                src: 'img/002.jpg',
                thumb_src: 'img/thumbs/002.jpg',
                title: 'Two'
            },
            {
                src: 'img/003.jpg',
                thumb_src: 'img/thumbs/003.jpg',
                title: 'Three'
            },
            {
                src: 'img/004.jpg',
                thumb_src: 'img/thumbs/004.jpg',
                title: 'Four'
            }
        ];
    },
    showImage: function($image) {
        var height = $(window).height() * 0.8;
```

```
            var width = $(window).width() * 0.8;
            var left = ($(window).width() / 2) - width / 2;
            var top = ($(window).height() / 2) - height / 2;
            var imgHeight = height * 0.8;
            var modalStyle = 'style="width: '+width+'px;
height:'+height+'px; left: '+left+'px; top: '+top+'px;"';
            var modal = '<div id="gallery-modal" class="modal">';
            modal += '<div class="overlay"></div>';
            modal += '<div class="modal-body" '+modalStyle+'>';
            modal += '<div class="modal-close" onclick="renderEngine.
removeModal()">X</div>';
            modal += '<h2>'+$image.attr('title')+'</h2><hr />';
            modal += '<img src="'+$image.attr('data-src')+'"
height="'+imgHeight+'" style="height:'+imgHeight+'px;
width:'+imgHeight+'px;"/>';
            modal += '</div>';
            modal += '</div>';
            $('body').append(modal);
        },
        removeModal: function() {
            var modal = document.getElementById('gallery-modal');
            $(modal).fadeOut(600);
            setTimeout(function(){
                $('.modal').remove();
            },700);
        }
    };
})(window, jQuery);
```

Now with that done, lets move to the index.html file and create the script that will trigger the functions that we just created.

Modify the opening <body> tag to look like this:

```
<body onload="renderEngine.init();">
```

This will initialize our renderEngine object so that it can be used throughout the rest of our document. Now let's put the code at the bottom of the page to use our renderEngine function.

Just before the ending of the `<body>` tag, add the following script:

```
$(document).ready(function() {
    if ($(window).width() > 720) {
        renderEngine.addGallery();
    } else {
        renderEngine.removeGallery();
    }
    $('.gallery-img').bind('click', function() {
        renderEngine.showImage($(this));
    });
});
```

The first `if` statement checks whether the window is greater than our break-point, `720` pixels. If it is, we render the gallery element in the DOM. After that, we bind the click event to the images in the gallery. You could even move this inside the if statement where the gallery will be created, as the event listener will not be needed if the gallery has not been created.

 Remember that a hidden image is still a rendered image.

It's important to remember that this principle can be applied to anything. If you have a responsive website that doesn't display columns on a mobile's viewport, use this idea to save load time.

Specifying sizes and media queries and introducing sprite sheets

Media queries allow us to create wonderful skeletons for our websites. If you build responsive websites, there is no doubt that you must come into contact with media queries. Here, we will cover some basics very quickly.

When you make use of media queries, always remember to include the viewport `<meta>` tag, which looks like this:

```
<meta name="viewport" content="width=device-width, initial-
scale=1">
```

The following content is taken from Mozilla Developers Network docs:

> *"If web developers want their scale settings to remain consistent when switching orientations on the iPhone, they must add a maximum-scale value to prevent this zooming, which has the sometimes-unwanted side effect of preventing users from zooming in:*

```
<meta name="viewport" content="width=device-width, initial-
scale=1, maximum-
scale=1">"
```

If you haven't already read it, I suggest that you read through the article at:

```
http://www.quirksmode.org/mobile/viewports2.html
```

It will help you to understand how viewports work and will make using media queries a lot easier.

Okay, so let's get started on media queries. Earlier in this chapter, I included a skeleton of media queries that I normally use to get started. I'll just include the break-points here again:

```
/* MOBILE */
@media screen and (max-width: 480px) {
    .container {
        width: 320px;
    }
}
/* TABLETS */
@media screen and (min-width: 481px) and (max-width: 720px) {
    .container {
        width: 480px;
    }
}
/* SMALL DESKTOP */
@media screen and (min-width: 721px) and (max-width: 960px) {
    .container {
        width: 720px;
    }
}
```

```
/* STANDARD DESKTOP */
@media screen and (min-width: 961px) and (max-width: 1200px) {
    .container {
        width: 960px;
    }
}
/* LARGE DESKTOP */
@media screen and (min-width: 1201px) and (max-width: 1600px) {
    .container {
        width: 1200px;
    }
}
/* EXTRA LARGE DESKTOP */
@media screen and (min-width: 1601px) {
    .container {
        width: 1600px;
    }
}
```

What this allows me to do is have a fixed-width container for the most popular viewport sizes and work with percentages from there. So, really it's a combination of adaptive and responsive designs. Responsive design is a lot more that just resizing a few HTML elements. If you haven't read the book, *Responsive Web Design, Ethan Marcotte*, you should probably do that, so that you will a deeper knowledge of responsive designing.

Caching

Caching images is a useful way to speed up the load time on your website. Your browser can save copies of images, style sheets, JavaScript files, or even entire web pages. Therefore, when the site requests the resource again, it does not need to be re-downloaded. There are various available caching options, which are as follows:

- Last-Modified
- ETag
- Expires
- Max-Age
- Public or Private

Each of these options is not specifically there for images. They will be covered in detail in the next chapter.

Scaling

One size fits all is certainly not a phrase I would use when it comes to responsive images. If you're loading a website on a smaller device, it just makes sense to use a smaller image. Sure, you could simply scale the image and resize it with the parent container, but why not load a smaller image that will speed up your load time and still look great?

A great little JavaScript plugin that you can use to achieve this is called `picturefill.js`. Let's look at an example.

The plugin is already included in the source files, so we can just modify the body content to get this working. This is illustrated in the following code:

```
<div class="container">
    <div class="header">
        <picture>
            <source srcset="img/large.jpg"
                    media="(min-width: 1200px)" />
            <source srcset="img/medium.jpg"
                    media="(min-width: 900px)" />
            <source srcset="img/small.jpg" />
            <!-- fallback -->
            <img src="img/small.jpg" alt="A rad wolf" />
        </picture>
    </div>
</div>
<!--[if IE]>
<script src="//cdnjs.cloudflare.com/ajax/libs/html5shiv/3.7.2/
html5shiv-printshiv.js"></script>
<![endif]-->
<!-- Include the Picture Polyfill -->
<script src="js/picturefill.min.js" async></script>
```

And voilà! That's it. The script makes use of the HTML5 picture element. Each source element contains a link to an image that will load at the declared minimum width of the viewport. In this example, there are three image sizes: small, medium, and large. It's worth mentioning that the `small.jpg` picture will always load, as this will be the default image, unless otherwise specified in the `media` tags.

This principle also applies to background images. In your media queries, change the background image source to use a smaller version for mobile devices, as less data means more speed.

You've just saved some data from being downloaded on your request and I can see your website viewers starting to smile already.

Retina displays

Since we live in a world where technology changes at a rapid pace, it's inevitable that techniques we use in our coding will become stale and limited. We have to start using hacks to make things work the way we want to or even just work at all. Media queries are no different, and they are becoming more complex with the addition of high-resolution displays such as retina displays.

Something might look great on your 1080p desktop screen, but on a hi-res retina display it may seem a bit out of proportion.

So, how do we circumvent this hindrance?

Chris Coyier, who is one of the founders of CodePen, has made a retina-ready media query example that looks like this:

```
@media
only screen and (-webkit-min-device-pixel-ratio: 2),
only screen and ( min--moz-device-pixel-ratio: 2),
only screen and ( -o-min-device-pixel-ratio: 2/1),
only screen and ( min-device-pixel-ratio: 2),
only screen and ( min-resolution: 192dpi),
only screen and ( min-resolution: 2dppx) {
    /* Retina-specific stuff here */
}
```

The first three conditions are not web standards but, for cross-compatibility, I would recommend using them. It will make your code a bit more future-proof.

 Please take not that Internet Explorer does not support dppx units.

Summary

Managing images is no small feat in a website. Almost all modern websites rely heavily on images to present content to the users.

In this chapter, we looked at which image formats to use and when. We also looked at how to optimize your images for websites. We discussed the difference between progressive and optimized images as well.

Conditional loading can greatly help you to load your site faster. In this chapter, we briefly discussed how to use conditional loading to improve your site's performance.

We touched on server-side optimization using cache and ETags and we considered media queries for retina displays.

4
Learning Content Management

Well! You've made it this far, so this chapter will treat you with plenty of examples and practical implementations of media queries, explaining technologies such as SASS, server-side optimizations, parallel downloads, and lots more.

Now that we're on the topic, let's consider this: what is meant by content management? It's not to be confused with content management systems such as WordPress, Joomla!, and the like. Well, what is it then? Content management simply means a process that manages your website's content served to the end users, with the end goal to improve their experience while using your product.

We've talked about this in the previous chapters when using technologies such as `picturefill.js` and conditional loading.

Where does content management originate from? What do we need to manage on a website? Well, mostly multimedia elements, pictures, videos, and audio, but that's not all. Your DOM elements are just as crucial, and over-downloading and over-rendering can have a negative impact on performance while using the website. When your jQuery script has 10 elements to transverse through as compared to 15 elements, you will see a decrease in your animation's performance and the responsiveness of interaction with elements. All this is bad!

Why is content management necessary? If it isn't obvious by now, then consider this: when offered to choose between a website that takes 10 seconds to load with a website that takes 2 seconds to load, you'd without a doubt prefer using the site that is loaded in 2 seconds. Also, if you click on a button and wait for 2 seconds for something to happen because your script isn't optimized, users will very quickly become frustrated. They will probably open the tab with their Facebook account and continue procrastinating because your product was not productive or efficient enough.

I'll admit that I'm a sucker for software products that look attractive. I'd rather use something that is more pleasing to the eye, especially if I'll be working with it on a regular basis. That being said, if a software product looks great but is really buggy and impractical, then I'd switch to something that works better. The same can be said about websites. If you build a website that looks amazing, and the layouts across all devices are fantastic, you'll still find it very difficult to build a user base if it doesn't work as your end users expect.

That's why design isn't enough, but neither is a good backend. You need a perfect mixture of both—something that is pleasing to look at and something that is a breeze to use. It's up to us as developers and designers to come together and create this perfect amalgamation of design, usability, and performance.

Style sheets, media queries, and viewports

We discussed style sheets, media queries, and viewports briefly in the previous chapters. Let's go into more detail and discuss techniques to use these to our advantage.

Implementing responsive design in a project takes a lot of careful planning. When done correctly, making use of responsive images and fluid grids can yield stunning, fast, and usable websites.

I strongly recommend reading through the W3C spec for media queries at `http://www.w3.org/TR/css3-mediaqueries/` to get a better understanding of the topic. They clearly document the features and how to handle errors.

Style sheets are a necessity for great websites. You can't build a professional website and place all of the CSS styling in your HTML page. Well, I guess you could, but that isn't very practical. Creating style sheets adds to the content the server needs to send the client, which means more things to download. One of the tools invented to help us out with this was minification, and it certainly makes a difference.

Another feature is the `@import` CSS function. Take a look at this example from Mozilla's developer pages:

```
@import url("fineprint.css") print;
@import url("bluish.css") projection, tv;
@import 'custom.css';
@import url("chrome://communicator/skin/");
@import "common.css" screen, projection;
@import url('landscape.css') screen and (orientation:landscape);
```

Rather than linking these style sheets in your <head> tag, you can import them directly into your main style sheet. This sounds great doesn't it? But there is one setback here: the style sheet importing these other style sheets will have to be parsed and executed before the browser knows it has to download other style sheets imported in this parent style sheet. This could, in fact, add a delay to the site's loading time, as the browser can no longer download these style sheets in parallel.

Sassy CSS, SASS, and LESS

Variables, calculations, and all sorts of fun tricks are some of the benefits made available when using SASS/SCSS.

Generally, when people talk about SASS, they'll be referring to the preprocessor and the language as a whole. The SASS preprocessor allows two syntaxes: SASS, an indented syntax, and SCSS, a CSS-like syntax.

SASS actually comes from another preprocessor, called **HAML**, that was designed and written by Ruby developers. Because of this, the SASS syntax is based on specific indentation and does not make use of semicolons. Take a look at this sample code to get better understanding of it. We'll compare CSS, SCSS, and SASS syntax in three examples.

CSS

Here is a piece of code that uses CSS:

```
.title-container {
    border-radius: 1.2em;
   -webkit-border-radius: 1.2em;
   -moz-border-radius: 1.2em;
    color: red;
    width: 100%;
    overflow: hidden;
}
.subtitle-container {
    border-radius: 1.5em;
   -webkit-border-radius: 1.5em;
   -moz-border-radius: 1.5em;
    color: orange
}
.content-container {
    border-radius: 2em;
```

```
    -webkit-border-radius: 2em;
    -moz-border-radius: 2em;
     color: orange;
}
```

SCSS

The following is a piece of code that utilizes SCSS:

```
// Declare the Variables
$main-colour: red;
$secondary-colour: orange
// Create a border radius Mixin
@mixin border-radius($radius) {
    -webkit-border-radius: $radius;
    -moz-border-radius: $radius;
    border-radius: $radius;
}
.title-container {
    color: $main-colour;
    width: 100%;
    overflow: hidden;
     @include border-radius(1.2em);
}
.subtitle-container {
    @include border-radius(1.5em);
     color: $secondary-colour;
}
.content-container {
    @include border-radius(2em);
    color: $seconday-colour;
}
```

SASS

Finally, here is a piece of code that uses SASS:

```
// Declare a Variable
!main-colour= red
!secondary-colour= orange
```

```
// Create a Mixin
=border-radius(!radius)
    border-radius= !radius
    -webkit-border-radius= !radius
    -moz-border-radius= !radius
.title-container
    color= !main-colour
    width= 100%
    overflow= hidden
    +border-radius(1.2em)
.subtitle-container

    +border-radius(1.5em)
    color= !secondary-colour
.content-container
    +border-radius(2em)
    color= !secondary-colour
```

You can clearly see the differences in the semantics of the three syntaxes. CSS is certainly the more manual of the three, whereas SASS requires the least amount of code to achieve the same results. This leaves SCSS in the middle.

One of the most useful features of both SCSS and SASS is the declaration of variables and `mixins`. Not only does it make your code more readable, but also maintaining it becomes much, much less of a pain. Let's say halfway through the project, someone decides that the secondary color will no longer be `orange` because it reminds them too much of a citrus fruit; it now has to change to yellow. If you used standard CSS, you'll have to skim through all of the code, find all the places where you set `orange` as the color, and change it manually. With both SCSS and SASS, you can simply change the variable, and when your CSS compiles, you will have changed all the instances of `orange` to yellow.

Okay, so all that is good fun! It helps you code more efficiently, and maintaining your style sheets becomes a lot simpler. Let's quickly take a look at installing SASS or SCSS on your computer.

Personally, I make use of CodeKit to assist with the development when I use SASS, as it comes preinstalled and is much easier to manage. If you're not using Mac OS X, I recommend using Compass.app. You can head over to `http://sass-lang.com/install` to get more information on the options available. SASS is cross-platform and can be used on Linux, Mac OS X, and Windows.

Let's pretend we've just received a new project about a new site and we want to use SASS in practice. Here is the design that the designer sent us:

Right, that's nice and simple! A heading with a subheading and an image. As developers, we pay attention to every little detail and plan everything carefully.

After some planning and lots of coffee, here is the markup I came up with:

```
<section class="origin-of-coffee">
    <header>
        <h2>The origin of coffee</h2>
        <h4>A man and his goat</h4>
    </header>
    <article>
        <img src="img/coffee.jpg" alt="a coffee plant" />
    </article>
</section>
```

I also included a reset style sheet, just to keep the styling more consistent across browsers. You can grab this from `http://meyerweb.com/eric/tools/css/reset/`. Essentially, you will be adding your own settings such as background color and so on, but for the purpose of this demo, I just used it as is.

Right, I think that's pretty good! Let's take a look at the result:

It's there, but it could use some prettifying.

All seems in place, so now, let's get cracking with some SASS. Start up your SASS compiler, be it CodeKit, Compass, or even via the terminal. Set the output file such that it will be put in a `css` folder and named `style.css`. The style sheet will be compiled in the `style.css` file, and that is the file we will link in our HTML.

Your `<head>` section should now look something like this:

```
<title>The origin of coffee</title>
<link rel="stylesheet" type="text/css" href="css/reset.css">
<link rel="stylesheet" type="text/css" href="css/style.css">
```

Of course, if you did not include a reset style sheet, there will be no link to it.

Now, this is the resulting SASS code that I went for. I added a `mixin` with multiple parameters, so it is very easy to reuse it on any element you would like to, as the following code shows:

```
// Defaults
$background:#c4c4c4
// Title
$title-size: 2em
$title-colour: #eee4cf
```

```
// Subtitle
$subtitle-size: 1.4em
$subtitle-colour: #f9f9f9

@mixin border-width($width, $style, $colour)
    border-width: $width
    border-style: $style
    border-color: $colour

body
    text-align: center
    background-color: $background
    font-family: Arial

.container
    margin: 0 auto

.headings
    padding: 15px 5px

.headings h2
    font-size: $title-size
    color: $title-colour
    margin-bottom: 7px

.headings h4
    font-size: $subtitle-size
    color: $subtitle-colour
    letter-spacing: 3px

.content img
    @include border-width(3px, solid, #FFF)
```

Easy peasy! Look how flexible this code is. The border-width mixin can be reused over and over. The colors can change whenever you want with a single modification, and all of this is automatically compiled in your style.css file. Another great function I like to create is a size function. This will allow you to pass two parameters, width and height. This is very handy when you work with a lot of images or box elements that need to be set to a specific size.

Let's take a peek at the result:

This seems almost right. It's a simple example, but it should give you some understanding of SASS.

Alright, you might be asking yourself, "what does all this have to do with responsive design? Did I start reading a different book?" The answer is "No." Here comes the best part. Take a look at this code snippet:

```
// Media Queries
$mobile-min: 320px
$mobile-max: 480px

.content img
    @include border-width(3px, solid, #FFF)
    @media screen and (max-width: $mobile-max)
        width: $mobile-min
```

That is a media query nested in a SASS declaration. At the top, you have your min and max values, and you can easily use these values in the styling to add breakpoints and all other fun things. Here is another one; let's take the same code snippet and add a math calculation:

```
$mobile-padding: 15px
.content img
    @include border-width(3px, solid, #FFF)
    @media screen and (max-width: $mobile-max)
        width: $mobile-min - $mobile-padding
```

This will compile to give the following code:

```
@media screen and (max-width: 480px) {
  .content img {
    width: 305px; }
}
```

You can easily substitute the fixed pixel values with percentage values and achieve fluid layouts with ease. When it comes to performance of your site, SASS is a performance booster for your productivity. The CSS rendered in your browsers has already been compiled, so when a site is rendered, the only real advantage SASS provides is that the CSS is minified.

LESS is a pure JavaScript CSS preprocessor that doesn't require the installation of Python. Many people would prefer this as some only need to have Python installed to use SASS. Why not rather use what you have?

LESS

Here is a nice description of LESS from their website:

Less is a CSS preprocessor, meaning that it extends the CSS language, adding features that allow variables, mixins, functions and many other techniques that allow you to make CSS that is more maintainable, themable and extendable.

Less runs inside Node, in the browser and inside Rhino. There are also many 3rd party tools that allow you to compile your files and watch for changes.

It is available from `http://lesscss.org`.

How does the code look, then?

Here is a sample taken from `http://lesscss.org`:

```
@base: #f938ab;

.box-shadow(@style, @c) when (iscolor(@c)) {
  -webkit-box-shadow: @style @c;
  box-shadow:         @style @c;
}
.box-shadow(@style, @alpha: 50%) when (isnumber(@alpha)) {
  .box-shadow(@style, rgba(0, 0, 0, @alpha));
```

```
}
.box {
  color: saturate(@base, 5%);
  border-color: lighten(@base, 30%);
  div { .box-shadow(0 0 5px, 30%) }
}
```

The preceding code will compile to give the following:

```
.box {
  color: #fe33ac;
  border-color: #fdcdea;
}
.box div {
  -webkit-box-shadow: 0 0 5px rgba(0, 0, 0, 0.3);
  box-shadow: 0 0 5px rgba(0, 0, 0, 0.3);
}
```

You can see from this sample that it shares similarities with SASS in the ability to declare variables and mixins. In the end, it'll be up to you to choose a preprocessor that you feel comfortable using.

Background images and media queries

We've taken a look at plugins such as `picturefill.js` for dynamic selection of varying images depending on the device size being used. This only affects HTML `img` elements. An often overlooked tweak is with background images.

The `background-size` property is very helpful for resizing background images on your page. However, like flexible images, this will still load the full-resolution image into your mobile and tablet devices. Not so great, right? Well, we know about media queries and we know about background images. So let's combine the two for a solution!

Consider this example:

```
.page {
    background: url('../img/page-bg.jpg');
}
```

Let's say `page-bg.jpg` is a beautiful, large, high-resolution image that we use on our website as a background for our page element. A div spans over the entire page. You can use a media query to resize the image using the `background-size` attribute, but that's exactly what you wouldn't want. This has no real advantage; surely, the image will appear responsive, but your download time is negatively affected.

So instead, use a separate image for tablets and use a media query to load it:

```css
@media screen and (max-width: 320px){
    .page {
        background: none !important;
    }
}

@media screen and (min-width:231px) and (max-width: 479px) {
    .page {
        background: url('../img/page-bg-mobile.jpg');
    }
}

@media screen and (min-width: 480px) and (max-width: 959px) {
    .page {
        background: url('../img/page-bg-tablet.jpg');
    }
}
```

With just a few lines of code we've saved a whole lot of bandwidth. Your end users will be smiling all the way to your website.

Using JavaScript to ease the load

In the previous chapter, we worked through an example using AJAX to populate content on the page to allow it to speed up a bit. In this section, we'll look at some JavaScript technologies that can help us speed up our website.

AngularJS

AngularJS is quickly becoming a popular **Single Page Application (SPA)** framework used to develop websites. Here is an explanation directly from one of AngularJS's documents:

AngularJS is a structural framework for dynamic web apps. It lets you use HTML as your template language and lets you extend HTML's syntax to express your application's components clearly and succinctly. Angular's data binding and dependency injection eliminate much of the code you would otherwise have to write.

Using SPAs makes your site feel a lot more like an app than a website. If you'd like to learn more about Angular, check out their official documentation at `https://code.angularjs.org/1.2.26/docs/guide/introduction`.

Conditional content management

We spoke about media queries to some extent, but there's even more. It's hard to believe, but I'm sure by the time you read this, there'll be even more!

So far, all the media query conditions we did were in a single CSS file. Another approach is to split the files for each query, as follows:

```
<link href="mobile.css" rel="stylesheet" media="screen and (max-width:
480px)" />
```

So, a typical `<head>` tag could look something like this:

```
<link href="small.css" rel="stylesheet" media="screen and (max-width:
480px)" />
<link href="medium.css" rel="stylesheet" media="screen (min-width:
481px) and (max-width: 720px)" />
<link href="desktop.css" rel="stylesheet" media="screen (min-width:
721px) and (max-width: 960px)" />
<link href="large.css" rel="stylesheet" media="screen (min-width:
961px) and (max-width: 1200px)" />
```

The server side with PHP

To load or not to load? Using a server-side language such as PHP has some wonderful benefits. The rendered content is already optimized and does not require JavaScript to remove unwanted elements, as it was not rendered earlier. In most cases, you are likely to use PHP only when connecting to a database to retrieve data or create new data. Another possible reason to use PHP is for sending an e-mail when posting a contact form, for example.

This section goes by the assumption that you have experience using PHP and have also connected to a database before, as this will not guide you through the steps to do so.

"If this then that; else, something else!" This is one of my favorite statements. When you use a framework such as CodeIgniter, this part becomes even more flexible.

Parallel downloads

Your web browser is pretty smart. It automatically makes as many connections as possible to the host to try and download content in parallel. Connections to a single host are limited, however. When a browser reaches the threshold, it puts other content in a queue. The content in the queue waits until other requests complete, and continues when more connections can be made. The time spent waiting for requests to finish is referred to as blocking. Our goal should be to reduce blocking as much as possible to achieve shorter load times.

One way by which you can improve parallel downloads is by using subdomains; for example, yoursite.com could have static.yoursite.com and static-img.yoursite.com. We call this domain sharing. Because you make more hosts available, more connections can be created and more content can be downloaded simultaneously. Your load times can dramatically improve because of this.

One thing to keep in mind is that some browsers don't download JavaScript files in parallel, so spreading those files across multiple hosts may yield no benefits. You should not take JS files into consideration when allocating resources to multiple hosts.

One of the best ways of reducing blocking is to reduce the content that needs to be downloaded. Make use of sprite sheets, combine your CSS wherever possible, and don't forget to minify.

 Some browsers do not download JavaScript files in parallel.

Content Delivery Networks

Content Delivery Networks (CDN) are an excellent way to improve the speed of your website.

What advantages does a CDN offer? Take a look at this diagram for a better understanding:

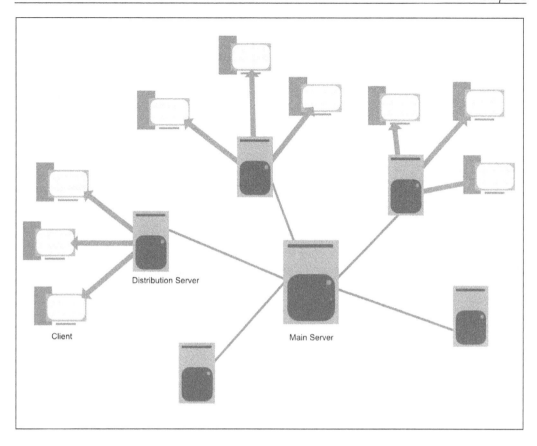

A CDN is an interconnected network of cache servers that use geographical proximity as a condition to deliver content to your client.

Multiple copies of the same content exist across multiple servers around the world, allowing the network to send the same content to multiple requesting clients effectively and reliably.

CDNs are well geared for delivering content such as audio, video, and even static web pages. A particular CDN's management dynamically calculates the distance between the requesting client and the servers, and selects the closest server in order to deliver content to the client. This reduces not only the distance the content has to travel but also the number of hops the packet needs to make to get to the requesting client.

Fonts

For as long as I can remember, pixels have been the unit of choice in web development. They're safe and easy to understand. Pixels are a set size and you know how big an image will be when you set them. But what happens when the viewport changes? Let's head over to the world of em and rem.

Using the em unit yields some advantages, but with it, there are also some complications. An em unit is relative to the size of its parent size setting. Let's say your body's font-size attribute is set to 100%:

```
body {
    font-size: 100%;
}
```

If you set a paragraph element nested immediately in the <body> tag to 1em, it will default to 16 pixels, assuming that the browser defaults have not been changed.

So, your HTML will look like this:

```
<body>
    <p>Hello, I am a paragraph set to 1em</p>
</body>
```

Your CSS style will look like the following:

```
body p {
    font-size: 1em;
}
```

The paragraph has now been set to 16 pixels. Had you set the paragraph to 2em, the size would have been 32 pixels. For this example to work, let's set the paragraph to 0.875em, which will set our font to 14 pixels. The easiest way to work with em is by using Ethan Marcotte's simple formula: *target ÷ context = result*.

So, in this case, we end up with *14 ÷ 16 = 0.875*.

Here's our new CSS:

```
body p {
    font-size: 0.875em;
}
```

Now, what does this mean for any child elements of the paragraph? Well, the context would change for child elements. You'll no longer use the `<body>` tag as the context, but the paragraph tag. Let's see how that works. First, add a `span` element to the paragraph, as shown here:

```
<body>
    <p>Hello, I am a paragraph set to 0.875em <span>and I'm a span</
span>
        </p>
</body>
```

Let's set the span to 12 pixels. Again, we're going to make use of that handy little formula: *target ÷ context = result*. With the new numbers, our context has changed: *12 ÷ 14 = 0.85714285714286*.

Now you might think, "Whoa! That number is way too long!" But fear not; your browser is more than capable of handling large numbers like this. Don't try to round it off, or else your browser will worry about that kind of stuff. You can just plug it in like this:

```
p span {
    font-size: 0,85714285714286em
}
```

You can probably imagine the complexities involved with a large website when using ems. Nested elements that constantly change context may quickly start causing headaches. Thus, rem (root em) came along. This is also relative, but its main advantage is that the context never changes. It always stays relative to the `<body>` tag's size setting. So, in the case of the `<span>` tag changing the context from 16 to 14 pixels, the context will remain 16 pixels and your result will look like this: *12 ÷ 16 = 0.75*.

Unfortunately, browser support for rem isn't as extensive as it should be in this day and age. Take a look at `http://caniuse.com/#feat=rem` for a list of supported browser versions to see whether you could use it in your project. As usual, Internet Explorer falls quite far behind when you choose anything older than version 9. Something to always keep in mind is browser compatibly. Whenever you make a change, test, test, and then test some more!

Summary

Getting to grips with content management will take your development in the right direction.

We took a look at style sheets, media queries, and working with viewports. We briefly covered the use of CSS preprocessors such as SASSY CSS, SASS, and LESS. Though these were not covered in detail, we wanted an introduction to help you find a starting point of investigation. CSS preprocessors are really an excellent way to code your style sheets, and once you get the hang of them, you can eliminate all lines of unnecessary code that you would've had to maintain otherwise. We also covered background images and media queries.

The web is slowly but surely moving towards an app-like experience, and frameworks such as AngluarJS are right at the forefront of this movement. Really, they're something worth taking a look at.

We touched on conditional content management with the `<link>` tag for loading style sheets as the specific device size requires.

Optimization doesn't occur only on the client side but sometimes on the server side as well. Sometimes, working on the server side to help deliver the correct content before it reaches the client is also an effective way of managing content.

Parallel downloads were briefly covered. You figured out that your web browser is pretty smart, and that it automatically makes as many connections as possible to the host to try and download content in parallel. We discussed the fact that the time the client spends waiting for requests to finish is referred to as blocking. Our goal should be to reduce blocking as much as possible to achieve shorter load time.

Another excellent way of delivering your sites quickly is by making use of content delivery networks. We mentioned what it is and how to make use of this.

The next topic we discussed was fonts and how it can affect your website's performance.

Alright, the next chapter we will discuss HTTP requests and how we can improve the loading time, sprite sheets image framing and a whole of other good practices that help reduce the number of requests made by the client to the server.

5
The Fastest HTTP Request is No HTTP Request

Until now, we have done a lot to reduce the time that spent loading your website. Surely, there's not much more that we can do? Well, yes, there is. I briefly mentioned reducing the number of HTTP requests in previous chapters but, this time, we will seriously improve the load time by making use of something that I call image framing. We will look at using sprites for buttons or background images by using inline images and will combine JavaScript files and some other server-side settings that can help us to improve performance.

Reducing the number of requests

In a previous chapter, I said that the bulk of load time is spent on loading images. So, we will start-off by focusing on reducing requests for images.

Sprite sheets

When you have a button or a background element such as Facebook, Twitter or any other link that you place on your website, you can very often reduce the number of requests by putting them in a sprite sheet.

Let's take this web page as our example:

Here is another website about coffee. I never get tired of this! This website has all the stuff that we need to improve HTTP requests: multiple images and buttons that are of the same size with different states. Let's just focus on the social media buttons. We have three buttons that are of the same size, 50 pixels by 50 pixels, and when you hover on a button, a darker version of that button is shown.

Now, instead of having six different images being fetched when a page is loaded, we are going to combine all the six images into sprite sheets.

So, what is a sprite sheet, anyway?

Most of us have played games before, so I'll use one of the most iconic games as an example to help explain sprite sheets. It's a me, Mario!

When programmers started developing 2D games, they needed a simple way to display animations. So, they must have thought, What would be better than making one image with a bunch of frames that the code can loop through? Here is Mario in his sprite sheet:

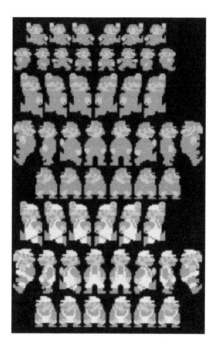

There he is, Mario, before programmers turned him into one of the most well-known game characters. You can clearly see the separate images, each forming part of an animation strip. In web development, we use the same concept, except, instead of using it for animations, we use it to reduce HTTP requests.

Take a look at this sprite sheet for our social buttons:

Using a sprite sheet like this, we instantly reduced the number of HTTP requests from six to one. That's quite significant and it's pretty simple to implement.

First things first; the HTML for our buttons will look like this:

```
<div class="button-container">
            <span class="btn-social btn-fb"></span>
            <span class="btn-social btn-tw"></span>
            <span class="btn-social btn-pt"></span>
</div>
```

By breaking it down, we will have three main parts: the button container that will house all the buttons, a main class for any social buttons, and a separate class for each button.

Now that we have this in place, it's time to make it look pretty.

The button container code looks like this:

```
.button-container {
  position: absolute;
  bottom: 0;
  height: 60px;
  width: 100%;
}
.button-container span {
  cursor: pointer;
}
.button-container span:hover {
  box-shadow: 0 2px 3px #000;
}
```

We position the buttons at the bottom of their parent container and set their height to be slightly larger than our 50 by 50 pixel buttons.

Then, just for appearance's sake, we set the cursor to show as a pointer and display a subtle drop shadow when you hover over each button.

Now, this is where the button styles come into play to help us display the sprite sheets, as shown in the following code:

```
.btn-social {
  display: inline-block;
  width: 50px;
```

```
    height: 50px;
    background-repeat: no-repeat;
    background-image: url("../img/social.jpg");
}
.btn-fb { /* facebook button */
    background-position: top left;
}
.btn-tw {/* twitter button */
    background-position: -50px 0;
}
.btn-pt {/* pintrest button */
    background-position: -100px 0;
}
.btn-fb:hover { /* facebook button */
    background-position: 0 -50px;
}
.btn-tw:hover {/* twitter button */
    background-position: -50px -50px;
}
.btn-pt:hover {/* pintrest button */
    background-position: -100px -50px;
}
```

Our main `btn-social` class sets up the default options for all the buttons. Since it's a `span` element, we need to set the display for the width and height for that element to have an effect. We set the display to `inline-block` and a fixed height and width of `50` pixels. Each image is `50` pixels high and `50` pixels wide. If you don't set the element to have the exact size of your image, you will run into display problems. So, it is advised that you use the same measurements for your element that you use for the actual button's size. Now, we have two more sections to look at: the individual buttons and their hover states.

Here, we will make use of the `background-image` and `background-position` attributes to show the frame of the image that we want to see on the screen.

Let's start with the Facebook button's default state.

We set the `background-image` attribute to use our sprite sheet that is named social. jpg. The most important value here is the `background-position` attribute. We set that as `top left`.

This will take the image and align it to the top-left hand corner. Since the element is set to be 50 by 50 pixels, it will only display the top-left image, the Facebook icon. Take a look at this for more clarity:

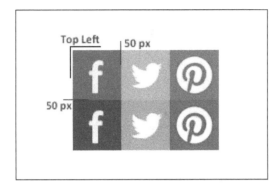

So, now we want to display the Twitter icon for our Twitter button. The same concept that we discussed earlier applies here as well. The background-position attribute will help us to position the image so that we see only the Twitter icon.

Let's set it to -50 pixels and 0 pixels. You may ask why not 50 pixels by 0 pixels? The minus sign pulls the image 50 pixels to the left. So, the first two number are for our left and right positioning, the negative number pulling the image to the left and the positive number pushing the image to the right. Again, our size is set to 50 pixels wide and 50 pixels high in the main btn-social class, so we will only see the section of the image that has our Twitter button.

Here is another screenshot to help make this clear:

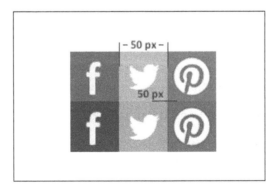

I think you get the idea. Now, the hover positioning is exactly the same for the left and right positions, but it changes slightly for the top alignment. The bottom frames are slightly darker than our top frames, so we need to pull the image 50 pixels upwards so that the middle 50-pixel point becomes our new zero. I mentioned that the first number in the `background-position` attribute is for the left and right position, so I guess it goes without saying that the second number will be for the top and bottom alignment.

So, here is how we achieve this:

```
.btn-fb:hover { /* facebook button */
   background-image: url("../img/social.jpg");
   background-position: 0 -50px;
}
```

This is simple, right? Yes, it is.

So remember, when you have a lot of small images, combine them into a sprite sheet to reduce the number of HTTP requests to a sensible number.

The next thing that I like to call "image framing" is something that I came up with. I'm sure that it has been used before by many other people, but I've decided to give it a name.

So, what is image framing?

Basically, **image framing** is a technique to use sprite sheets with `<img>` tags. It's actually quite a simple process.

Image framing consists of three main parts: a container element, a frame element nested in the container, and an image element that is nested in the frame. Therefore, the name: image framing.

The beauty of image framing is its ability to use larger images as sprite sheets. I wouldn't recommend images larger than 1,000 pixels, as this could make your file size unreasonably large.

So, how would this work in practice? Let's take our example from the previous section and use the two images to create a single sprite sheet, as shown in the following screenshot:

- A container element
- A frame
- An image

Let get going by creating the HTML code for our image, as shown in the code snippet:

```
<div class="container">
    <!-- Image one -->
    <div class="imgContainer">
        <img class="imgOne" src="img/map.jpg" alt="Image map"/>
        <div class="button-container">
            <span class="btn-social btn-fb"></span>
            <span class="btn-social btn-tw"></span>
            <span class="btn-social btn-pt"></span>
        </div>
    </div>
    <!-- Image Two -->
    <div class="imgContainer">
        <img class="imgTwo" src="img/map.jpg" alt="Image map"/>
        <div class="button-container">
            <span class="btn-social btn-fb"></span>
            <span class="btn-social btn-tw"></span>
            <span class="btn-social btn-pt"></span>
        </div>
    </div>
</div>
```

If we break down the code, we see that the container is our container (I'm sure you knew this already), the img-frame will be our frame, and the `<img>` tag will be, well, the image.

Here is the sprite sheet for this page:

The original image is 600 pixels wide by 750 pixels tall. That's not too large at all and, since it's a JPEG image, the size is very reasonable indeed. Now, how do we use image framing? We have created the HTML skeleton, but now we need to use CSS to make it into a pretty website.

This CSS code is as follows:

```
.container {
  width: 960px;
  margin: 0 auto;
  text-align: center; }
```

The container itself is very straightforward. Set a default width, put the content in the centre, and that's it. We will use some media queries to resize our content. The next thing that we will look at is the frame, which is actually the important bit:

```
.img-frame {
  overflow: hidden;
  height: 375px;
  width: 600px;
  position: relative;
  border: 1px solid #FFF;
  margin: 10px auto; }
```

You might notice that the `overflow` attribute is set as `hidden`. This will allow us to do exactly what we did with our sprite sheets when we set the background position and element size. Any content that is larger that the size of the frame will be cut off. In addition, note that the position is set to relative; this is also very important for positioning the child elements (the images) in the frame. The next thing that we will look at is the images:

```
.img-frame img {
  position: absolute;
  display: inline-block;
  width: 100%; }

.imgOne {
  top: 0;
  left: 0; }

.imgTwo {
  top: -375px;
  left: 0; }
```

By default, the images will be set with the position attribute as absolute value. In this way, we can manipulate the top and left attributes of the image. The width:100% setting will come into action when we start with our media queries, as the image needs to be flexible when the frame size changes.

The magic happens in the imgOne and imgTwo classes. The first image is positioned to be aligned at the top-left corner of the image. The height of the frame is set to 375 pixels and, because of the overflow: hidden attribute, any part of our image over 375 pixels will be cut off, like an image in a frame. This is great, but you might want to make this responsive, which is easy as pie!

Here is a snippet of code that I wrote to make the page responsive:

```
/* MOBILE */
@media screen and (max-width: 480px) {
  .container {
    width: 320px;
  }
  .imgContainer {
    @include setWidth(300px);
    height: 185px;
    margin: 10px 0;
  }
  .imgTwo {
    top: -187px;
  }
}
/* TABLETS */
@media screen and (min-width: 481px) and (max-width: 720px) {
  .container {
    width: 480px;
  }
  .imgContainer {
    @include setWidth(475px);
    height: 295px;
    margin: 10px 0;
  }
```

```
    .imgTwo {
      top: -297px;
    }
}
/* SMALL DESKTOP */
@media screen and (min-width: 721px) and (max-width: 960px) {
    .container {
      width: 720px;
    }

}
/* STANDARD DESKTOP */
@media screen and (min-width: 961px) and (max-width: 1200px) {
    .container {
      width: 960px;
    }
}
/* LARGE DESKTOP */
@media screen and (min-width: 1201px) and (max-width: 1600px) {
    .container {
      width: 1200px;
    }
}
/* EXTRA LARGE DESKTOP */
@media screen and (min-width: 1601px) {
    .container {
      width: 1600px;
    }
}
```

All I really needed to do to make the image framing responsive was adjust the width and height of the frame and change the top position of the second image. The first image will always have a position of top-left with the top attribute as 0 value and the left attribute as 0 value.

If you want to add any effects, such as box-shadow, to the image, you can add the styles to the image frame. Since the image frame is set to a fixed height and width and contains the image, it will reflect the styles on the image. Here is an example of a box-shadow set on the frame:

A simple page with three requests and what looks like eight different images. I think this qualifies as pretty efficient.

To conclude, image framing is a great way to reduce HTTP requests for larger images. This is best used in a scenario where all the images in the sprite sheet are used on the page that is displayed.

If you're requesting a sprite sheet but you will make use of only one image on it, it would be certainly more efficient to only download the one image that will be displayed rather than a sprite sheet that won't confer any benefit.

Combining files

Now that we can reduce the number of images that we request, why don't we reduce the resources that we use as well? Fewer files means a faster website.

When I started developing websites, I often requested two, three, or even four CSS files from the server. It never even crossed my mind to combine these files into one minified kilobyte-sized file. There isn't much here to do as the concept speaks for itself. When you use an application such as CodeKit or Compass.app, it is even easier to do this.

Your media queries and styles can all be in one file. A good practice is to split up the media queries and the main styles. If you're following the mobile-first methodology, you most probably do your mobile styles first and use the media queries to expand on your design, rather that diminishing your styles, and so on, in media queries.

The negative side of this is that, if you combine too many files, you could delay loading the rest of the website. So, find a balance between combining files and reasonable load times.

JavaScript files can also be combined and minified to save requests. Minified JavaScript files will also reduce the size, allowing content to be downloaded faster. Making use of CDNs is also a great way to help speed up the downloading of your JavaScript resource.

You should always avoid scattering your JavaScript code on separate HTML files and create a global JavaScript file.

Server-side optimization with Apache

Improving your website's speed is not only limited to reducing requests, managing images, or using fancy plugins to make your work easier. There are a lot of available options for improving website performance on your server.

Your best friend is an HTML boilerplate. If you haven't taken a look at this yet, you should make an effort to see how it does things.

Head over to `http://www.initializr.com` to build your own custom boilerplate template. The responsive template is an old favorite of mine. If you find it easier to use bootstrap styling, you can opt for the bootstrap template.

Another widely popular solution is to make use of Yeoman. This is a tiny library that you can install on your computer and it download all kinds of boilerplate framework libraries. For more information on this, head over to `http://yeoman.io`.

You will see there that it doesn't just include web scaffolding, there are even projects such as Ionic Framework for mobile development. It is definitely worth checking out. Head over to their generator page at `http://yeoman.io/generators/` to see what they have to offer.

Apache performance improvements can be found in the `.htaccess` file that you place in your website. Point your browser to `https://github.com/h5bp/html5-boilerplate` and navigate to the dist folder. There you will find the `.htaccess` file. Open it and then let's start looking at it.

Scroll down to WEB PERFORMANCE.

This section is divided into Compression, ETags, Expires Headers, File concatenation, and lastly, Filename-based cache busting.

Let's break down each of these and take a look at why we would use these.

Compression

Using compression on your content can minimize the size of the content being delivered. This is done by compressing it when it is being transferred from the server and deflating it when it arrives at the client location. This is done by the following code line:

```
<IfModule mod_deflate.c>
```

The preceding piece of code checks whether the module to compress/deflate the content is currently enabled on the server.

You might wonder if compression has a notable effect on your website? Take a look at this screenshot that I took from a website using GZIP compression.

As you can see from the screenshot, the website file size was reduced by **76.6**%, which is more than half its original size. A great place to test the compression is to go to `http://www.feedthebot.com/tools/gzip/` and enter your web URL.

If you're using a NGINX server, the code will be slightly different; here is a sample:

```
gzip on;
gzip_comp_level 2;
gzip_http_version 1.0;
gzip_proxied any;
gzip_min_length 1100;
gzip_buffers 16 8k;
gzip_types text/plain text/html text/css application/x-javascript
text/xml application/xml application/xml+rss text/javascript;

# Disable for IE < 6 because there are some known problems
gzip_disable "MSIE [1-6].(?!.*SV1)";

# Add a vary header for downstream proxies to avoid sending cached
gzipped files to IE6
gzip_vary on;
```

ETags

An article on ETags by Yahoo developers at `https://developer.yahoo.com/blogs/ydn/high-performance-sites-rule-13-configure-etags-7211.html`, states that:

> *"Entity tags (ETags) are a mechanism that web servers and browsers use to determine whether the component in the browser's cache matches the one on the origin server. (An "entity" is another word a "component": images, scripts, style sheets, etc.) ETags were added to provide a mechanism for validating entities that is more flexible than the last-modified date. An ETag is a string that uniquely identifies a specific version of a component. The only format constraints are that the string be quoted. The origin server specifies the component's ETag using the ETag response header."*

ETags are very handy in conjunction with caching. It compares the item in cache and then redownloads it if it has changed. It also prevents the content from getting stuck in the cache when it needs to change.

Expires headers

Let's say you have a website and it loads 50 resources. How terrible would it be if, every time a user returns to the website, all 50 resources had to redownload every time. That's not ideal. Fortunately, we have the ability to cache resources.

For static content, such as JavaScript files, favicons, and other content that will not change very often, it's safe to set a long expiry. This way, when the website is accessed, these items will be in cache, and this will automatically make the website faster for your users.

File concatenation

Combining JavaScript manually is effective, but it is quite a tedious task. So, here is a great way to make this a little easier.

As an example, if you have a JavaScript file called `main.js`, you can include other JavaScript file contents in the main file by using an include statement. Here is an example:

```
#include file="js/jquery.js"
```

If file concatenation has been enabled on the server, the contents of `jquery.js` will be inserted into the `main.js` file.

You can make use of a tool available from `http://yui.github.io/yuicompressor/` for this. There is also Grunt or Gulp that you can use to automate both file concatenation and CSS minifying. Both of these are task runners. They allow you to automate your web development. Both are very well-supported and have plenty of documentation as well.

AppCache

Another excellent way to reduce requests is to use AppCache. You can find an introduction to get the hang of what AppCache is by visiting `http://www.html5rocks.com/en/tutorials/appcache/beginner/`.

As listed on the website, here are the three advantages of making use of AppCache:

- **Offline browsing**: Users can navigate your full website when they're offline
- **Speed**: Resources come straight from the user's disk with no trip to the network
- **Resilience**: If your website goes down for "maintenance" (as in, someone accidentally breaks everything), your users will get the offline experience

Summary

One of the best ways to improve the load time of your website is by reducing requests. We took a look at some effective and easy-to-implement techniques to help you achieve speedy load times. We discussed sprite sheets and how they take a bunch of requests and turn them into one request. The next topic that we touched on was combining files.

Server-side optimization is also a great place to make some improvements. It makes use of compression to decrease the size of your content being received from the server.

We talked about some more server-side optimization, and then we mentioned AppCache, which is another excellent method to improve your website's performance.

In the next chapter, we will talk about a very important topic; testing.

6
Testing, Testing, and Testing!

From the heading of this chapter, I believe you've understood that we'll be talking about testing—lots of it. One of the most important, and often overlooked, parts of your work is testing. If you work on a project and, halfway through, realize that you have implemented something incorrectly, it could turn out to be catastrophic if you have to change the way it works.

The golden rule I follow is to use an agile method for projects and testing.

If any new feature, no matter how small, is added, I test everything to make sure I didn't override or break something else.

Giving a product that isn't functioning as it should to a client is a terrible thing to do. You need to ensure that you have tested it as much as possible.

Beginning your testing adventure

One of the first steps in the testing process is planning. If you don't know what you'll be testing, then how would you know what results to expect?

Let's break the testing process down into a few simple steps and make it as efficient as possible. Going by these steps will make the process of managing your project simpler as well. It's good to keep a record of your testing. When something does go wrong, and you missed it, you can easily go back to your testing data and evaluate what could have caused the problem to arise.

There are different types of testing. Test-driven development is a well-known approach to the development process. Here is a simple diagram that explains the workings of test-driven development or TDD:

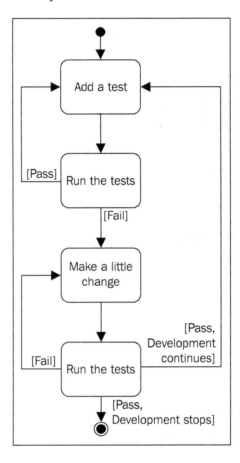

Step 1 – planning

Know what you want to test, and know what results you expect from each test. Defining tests, and the results for the tests, is the best way to get accurate test data.

Define each test with a set of required actions and outputs. As an example, let's take logging in to a website as our first test. Here is a sample screenshot showing the login page:

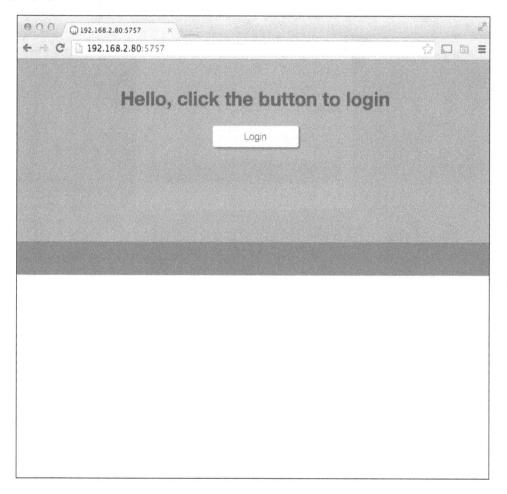

After clicking on the **Login** button present on the home screen, we get the **Login** testing page, as shown in the following screenshot:

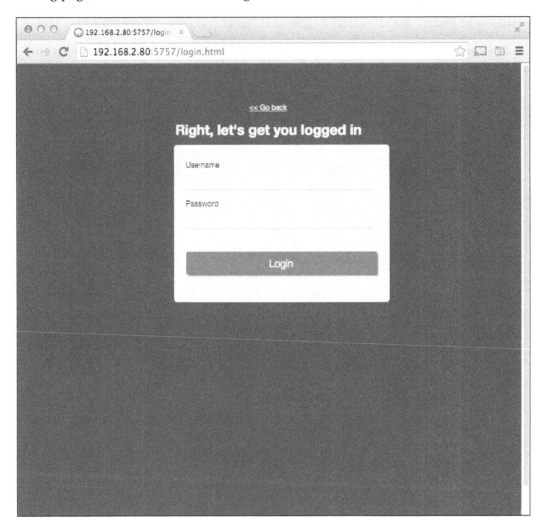

Let's make a quick summary of the actions in this case. It is as simple as the following:

1. Click to open the login page.
2. Enter the name and password.
3. Click on the **Login** button.

Now that we have determined what actions will be tested, let's decide how we will evaluate the output of our actions.

Your expected output evaluation can be defined, as follows:

- Opening the page:
    - Responsiveness of the **Login** button
    - Time spent loading the login page

- Entering the name and surname (this is pretty straightforward and does not require any real output):
    - Is the validation of the username and password accurate?

- Clicking on the login button:
    - Is the login button responsive?
    - Does the validation cater for empty values?
    - Is visual feedback displayed when the button is clicked on?

Step 2 – testing

The next step will be to actually perform the tests described in your planning. Open the page, click on the **Login** button, and use the tools at your disposal to evaluate the speed. Make notes as you go along. Most modern web browsers come with wonderful tools to help you evaluate your website's performance and manage errors that you may need to pay attention to. When looking at the speed and response of your interactions, the waterfall chart in your developer panel is a great place to start.

Step 3 – assessing results

Now that you have gone through the process of testing your page, you need to assess the results. Has your user interface responded in a timely fashion? Did the page load in an acceptable period of time? Write down all of this in a table outlining your testing. Give each action a pass or fail with a reason. This will help you build a record and allow you to easily add items to your bug list. Note that you should always have a bug list.

Step 4 – tracking bugs

Right, now that you've assessed your actions along with their output, it's time to take the items that have failed to the bug list. Keeping a bug list is crucial for bigger projects. You can never have too much information about the project.

As you squash your bugs, remember to reward yourself by checking them off the list, and perhaps treat yourself to a cup of coffee. There are many options available for keeping track of your development. Git offers a great solution whereby you can keep documentation, track bugs, and use source control.

Now you realize the previously mentioned steps are not aimed at responsive design, but rather at project management. This is still a great habit to pick up and will help both your responsive web projects and any other projects you might take on to become a lot more manageable.

So, remember the four steps of basic testing:

1. Planning.
2. Testing.
3. Assessing.
4. Tracking.

Back to the responsive stuff

Okay, so you would obviously like me to carry on and talk more about responsive web design performance testing.

Each developer has their preferred set of applications, or tools, that they use to work with, and testing is no different. There are literally hundreds of tools to choose from. One of the most basic things you have to become familiar with is the waterfall chart. It will be a great asset when you develop and test your web site.

Some other great tools to make use of are online web testing, viewport previewers, and speed-testing tools

Let's start with speed-testing tools. One of my favorite tools is actually made by the search and advertising giant, Google. You can get the add-on from the Chrome App Store or, if you're not using Chrome, you can access the online version at `https://developers.google.com/speed/pagespeed/insights/`.

Here is a screenshot of a sample result from a website:

You can see a clear analysis of your website in the two tabs. It even gives you links to help you fix the detected issues. Very helpful indeed!

Another tool that goes hand in hand with Google's **PageSpeed Insights** is WebPageTest, which you can find at `http://www.webpagetest.org`.

The result set of this page is a bit more involved and technical. The following screenshot shows a sample of the same site from the **PageSpeed Insights** test:

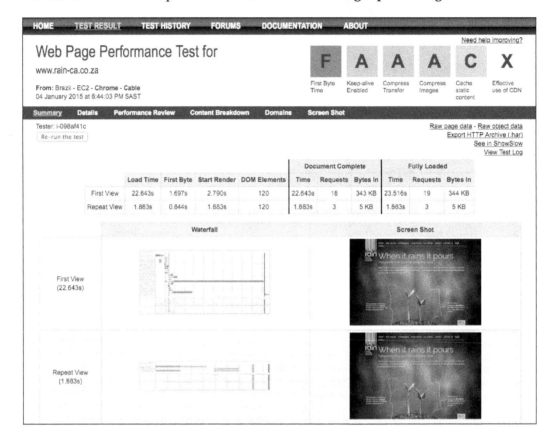

You immediately see a difference in the results; WebPageTest is a lot more involved and gives you considerably more detailed information.

Another great asset in your testing arsenal is seeing your website in different viewports. Not everybody is lucky enough to have one example of every device to test on. So many of us have to rely on resizing the browser, which is also not ideal. Therefore, the next best thing is to use a tool that can help you view your responsive website as it would appear on a mobile device, such as a phone or tablet.

If you're a Chrome user, you may (or may not) have already discovered the gem hidden in the Developer Console.

If you open the Developer Console by pressing either *F12* on Windows or *Alt + Cmd + i* on Mac OS X, you will see a tiny icon that looks like a phone in the top-left corner of the console, as shown in the following screenshot:

When you click on that button, it will open Chrome's device mode. There, you can select the type of device, or even a custom resolution at which you want your site to display.

Firefox has a tool called **Responsive Design** view. There are three ways you can enable Firefox's **Responsive Design** view:

- Select the **Responsive Design** view from the **Web Developer** submenu in Firefox (or the **Tools** menu if you see the menu bar or are using OS X)
- Press the **Responsive Design** view button in the toolbox's toolbar
- Press *Ctrl + Shift + M* (*Cmd + Opt + M* on OS X)

Finally, there is working with waterfall charts. Waterfall charts are a visual representation of how the website is built piece by piece, where the pieces come from, and how long it takes to fetch each piece. They can be found in your browser's developer tools, usually under the **Network** tab.

Here is a screenshot of a waterfall chart from `http://www.cnn.com`:

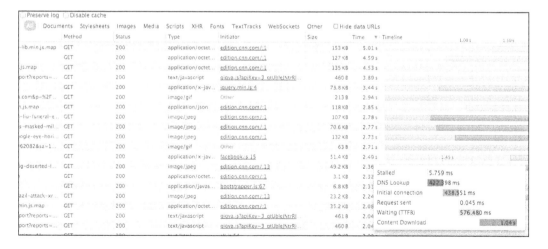

This is a tiny snippet from the chart, just to illustrate its different sections.

To the left is the name of the document, style sheet, script, or network request being fetched. The next column is the request method, GET or POST. The status is the HTTP status code of the request. The type column specifies the type of file being requested. It is followed by the initiator column, which tells you from where the request is being sent. The last three columns can be resized, as it suggests; Size displays the size of the file, Time is the total time spent fetching the file, and, finally, Timeline is a visual representation of the request.

The timeline is divided into a few parts. Hovering over the bar brings up a detailed display of the request that you can use to determine where your load time is being lost.

There are a lot of tools available to make your testing easier, and becoming aquatinted with the tools available will help you in the long run:

- `http://www.guypo.com/performance-implications-of-responsive-design-book-contribution/`
- `http://mobiletestingfordummies.tumblr.com`

Summary

I'm pretty sure that, by now, you've noticed I keep telling you: testing, testing, and more testing. So, I guess there is no reason to say it again here. Maybe, just once more—when you develop, make sure you do testing, testing, and some more testing!

Your basic test plan should include your deadlines, budget, and assessments of what would be a realistic goal. You should keep track of your changes via documentation and be sure that you have some sort of source control in your project.

In the next chapter, we will discuss the design concepts that can be followed to help improve a site's performance.

7
Speeding Up Development with Design Concepts, Patterns, and Programs

You're still here! This chapter will talk about design concepts such as mobile first, will give you better understanding of object-oriented CSS (OOCSS), and will touch on some patterns that you can use to make yourself more productive and improve your site's overall maintainability and performance.

Design concepts

One of the most popular design concepts is mobile first. It's not a new notion at all. Mobile first has been around for quite a few years. One of the accelerators of the mobile first principle was the announcement by Eric Schmit, from Google, in 2010 that Google will be taking the mobile first approach from then on. There is an article about this announcement that you can check out at `http://www.telegraph.co.uk/technology/google/7256103/Google-now-a-mobile-first-company.html`.

Graceful degradation and progressive enhancement

With mobiles becoming all the rage, two approaches were developed from the need to diversify and make your site look great on mobile and desktop. We will look at the two approaches, with an explanation and a simple example to clearly illustrate the difference between the two.

First, we have graceful degradation. Graceful degradation is an approach to building a working website that functions with a certain level of user experience in modern browsers, but will gracefully degrade in user experience levels as older browser features become unavailable. The basic level of functionality is not as nice as the full feature set, but at least things don't break!

Then we have progressive enhancement. Progressive enhancement is quite similar, but it does things the other way round. Your starting point is figuring out what basic level of user experience all browsers will be able to provide for your project when displaying your website. Then you can continue to build advanced functionality, and it will become available to browsers that do support it.

To summarize, graceful degradation starts with all the features modern browsers support and tries to fix them for browsers that don't support the new features, whereas progressive enhancement starts with the most basic set of features for your project and extends those features as they become available.

Okay, now that we know what the differences are, let's take a look at them in practice.

Printing booking results for a room you have booked in a hotel is something that you can't achieve in HTML. You need JavaScript to add this functionality. The problem is that, if your JavaScript is disabled or your browser doesn't support printing (for example, if it is a mobile phone), your user is faced with a button that doesn't do anything. Buttons that don't do anything produce a terrible user experience, as users might feel cheated out of something that they where offered!

Here is a basic implementation of a print button:

```
<p id="printthis">
  <a href="javascript:window.print()">Print this page</a>
</p>
```

We added a pseudo JavaScript protocol. As mentioned, this will work just fine if JavaScript is enabled and the browser supports printing. A slightly better approach would be something like this:

```
<p id="printthis">
  <a href="javascript:window.print()">Print this page</a>
</p>
<noscript>
  <p class="scriptwarning">
    Printing the page requires JavaScript to be enabled.
    Please turn it on in your browser.
  </p>
</noscript>
```

Using the `<noscript>` tag causes a message to be displayed when JavaScript is not enabled. One of the problems with this approach is that you assume a few things about your users. The assumptions are as follows:

- They know what JavaScript is
- They know how to enable it
- They have the permissions to change settings in their browser
- They are okay with turning on JavaScript to print a document

So, how can we make this a bit better? Use the following code:

```
<p id="printthis">
  <a href="javascript:window.print()">Print this page</a>
</p>
<noscript>
  <p class="scriptwarning">
    Print a copy of your confirmation.
    Select the "Print" icon in your browser,
    or select "Print" from the "File" menu.
  </p>
</noscript>
```

Now we've solved the JavaScript problem, but we still assume a few things. They are as follows:

- All browsers have the same printing functionality
- The menu structure is the same across all browsers

The overall problem with this approach, however, is more substantial. We start by offering a functionality that we fully know might not be available across all devices and browsers. Then we end up requiring to explain why the feature doesn't work as the user expects it to.

If we take the progressive enhancement approach, we have to consider a few limitations first. We mentioned them in the preceding example. Firstly, we can't assume that the user has JavaScript enabled and that the browser has the functionality to print. So, instead of assuming these things, let's provide the basics:

```
<p id="printthis">Thank you for your order. Please print this page for
your records.</p>
```

We tell the user that they must print the document, but we leave the *how* up to them. Next, let's write a script that extends the functionality as it becomes available:

```
<p id="printthis">Thank you for your order. Please print this page for
your records.</p>
<script type="text/javascript">
(function(){
  if(document.getElementById){
    var pt = document.getElementById('printthis');
    if(pt && typeof window.print === 'function'){
      var but = document.createElement('input');
      but.setAttribute('type','button');
      but.setAttribute('value','Print this now');
      but.onclick = function(){
        window.print();
      };
      pt.appendChild(but);
    }
  }
})();
</script>
```

This script is quite defensive and assumes nothing, for the sake of the user.

We put the code in an anonymous function so that the code executes on its own, making it unobtrusive as far as the rest of your is concerned code.

Firstly, we test DOM support by checking whether `document.getElementById` exists. Then we try to get the element and again check whether that element exists and whether the window supports printing. Only then do we continue to use JavaScript to add a button that will execute the print function when its click event has fired.

The progressive enhancement approach doesn't require any explanations as to why the feature doesn't work as expected. When browsers get updated with the new features, they will become available on your site.

Object-oriented CSS (OOCSS)

A lot of people stand by the principle that "content is king." Images, videos, and interactive content rule your website. I don't disagree with this at all, but speed is also just as important. If you have a slow website, chances are that people won't see your interactive content anyway.

When optimization occurs, most people start with JavaScript—it's not a bad place, but CSS often gets overlooked. So let's talk about object-oriented CSS and how it will help improve the performance and maintainability of your site.

The core principle of OOCSS is to focus not only on reusable code but also on faster and more maintainable style sheets.

OOCSS is based on two main principles. Let's discuss these two principles and what they mean.

Separating structure from styling

Separating the structure from the styling or skinning abstracts the structure of an element from its position and styling. When you abstract these elements, they become modules that can be reused across your website. You can apply the structure module to an element and expect the same type of result.

Take a look at the following snippet of CSS styling before separating the structure from the style:

```
#btn {
    /* Dimensions */
    width: 200px;
    height: 48px;
    padding: 7px;
```

```
    /* Style */
    border: solid 1px #ccc;
    background: linear-gradient(#ccc, #222);
    box-shadow: rgba(0, 0, 0, .5) 2px 2px 5px;
}

#bubble {
    /* Dimensions */
    width: 400px;
    border-radius: 50%;
    /* Style */
    overflow: hidden;
    border: solid 1px #ccc;
    background: linear-gradient(#ccc, #222);
    box-shadow: rgba(0, 0, 0, .5) 2px 2px 5px;
}

#widget {
    /* Dimensions */
    width: 500px;
    min-height: 200px;
    /* Style */
    overflow: auto;
    border: solid 1px #ccc;
    background: linear-gradient(#ccc, #222);
    box-shadow: rgba(0, 0, 0, .5) 2px 2px 5px;
}
```

If you look closely, you can see that all three elements share the same properties in `background` and `box-shadow`. Not only that, they are also applied using the non-resumable ID (#) selector. Let's separate the styles from our structure, as shown in the following CSS code:

```
.btn {
    width: 200px;
    height: 50px;
}

.bubble {
    width: 400px;
```

```
    border-radius: 50%;
    overflow: hidden;
}

.widget {
    width: 500px;
    min-height: 200px;
    overflow: auto;
}

.style {
    border: solid 1px #ccc;
    background: linear-gradient(#ccc, #222);
    box-shadow: rgba(0, 0, 0, .5) 2px 2px 5px;
}
```

It's easy to see that your code is now a lot more reusable. Each element has a class to define its dimensions or extra settings, and the styles that were shared have been moved to a .style class. You can apply this .style class to any element that requires this style.

Separating the containers and the content

If you read through the OOCSS GitHub wiki page, you will see that the second principle is the separation of the containers and the content. Let's take a look at the next piece of CSS:

```
#header p {
    font-weight: 300;
    line-height: 1.1em;
    color: #CCC;
    margin 5px auto;
    padding: 0;
}
```

The preceding piece of CSS isn't incorrect by any means. This style would apply to any paragraph element that is a child of the #header container. So what would happen to our CSS should we want to apply the same styling to another paragraph section? We could end up with something like the following:

```
#header p, #content p {
    font-weight: 300;
    line-height: 1.1em;
```

```
    color: #CCC;
    margin 5px auto;
    padding: 0;
}
#content p {
    line-height: 1.3em;
    color: #FFF;
    padding: 5px 0px;
}
```

In the worst-case scenario, we could do something like this:

```
#header p, {
    font-weight: 300;
    line-height: 1.1em;
    color: #CCC;
    margin 5px auto;
    padding: 0;
}
#content p {
    font-weight: 300;
    line-height: 1.1em;
    margin 5px auto;
    line-height: 1.3em;
    color: #FFF;
    padding: 5px 0px;
}
```

Look at all that code duplication. More lines of code means bigger file size, bigger file size means a longer download time, and a longer download time means a slower website. I think you've got the picture. This might not seem like a big thing but, when you want to focus on the performance of your website, every kilobyte makes a difference.

To know more about this, take a look at some of the work Nicole Sullivan has done. One of her contributions to the OOCSS movement is media objects. A link that is worth reading, and an explanation on saving plenty of lines of code, is at `http://www.stubbornella.org/content/2010/06/25/the-media-object-saves-hundreds-of-lines-of-code/`.

OOCSS and SASS/SCSS (even LESS)

Even though object-oriented CSS is brilliant, it does have a downside. Let's say you have strictly followed the OOCSS principles, your HTML will become littered with CSS classes. If you had to change this at some stage, you might find yourself crawling through your HTML code to find all those classes you added to your elements.

So, a great way to make your CSS more maintainable and still stick to OOCSS is to use CSS with SASS.

CSS is quite non-semantic. Look at this snippet:

```
<a class="btn-blue light-border">Facebook</a>
<a class="btn-lightblue light-border">Twitter</a>
```

It should actually be semantic:

```
<a class="facebook-btn">Facebook</a>
<a class="twitter-btn">Twitter</a>
```

The CSS for the semantic version would look something like this:

```
.facebook-btn {
    width: 150px;
    height: 47px;
    padding: 5px;
    border-radius: 3px;
    color: #FFF;
    background-color: #3b5998;
    border: thin solid #CCC;
}
.twitter-btn {
    width: 150px;
    height: 47px;
    border-radius: 3px;
    padding: 5px;
    color: #FFF;
    background-color: #55acee;
    border: thin solid #CCC;
}
```

No so great! Styles are duplicated everywhere. Okay, so let's align the code with our OOCSS principles:

```
<a class="btn lightborder facebook-btn">Facebook</a>
<a class="btn lightborder twitter-btn">Twitter</a>
```

Now we end up with something like this:

```
.btn {
    padding: 5px;
    border-raduis: 3px;
    color: #FFF;
}
.light-border: {
    border: thin solid #CCC;
}
.facebook-btn {
    background-color: #3b5998;
}
.twitter-btn {
    background-color: #55acee;
}
```

Okay, so your code is following OOCSS, which is great, but your CSS classes are not semantic and all of your extending happens in your HTML file, leaving your HTML filled with class names.

Let's use a `mixin` effect to create semantic markup for those two buttons. The HTML code required is as follows:

```
<a class="facebook-btn">Facebook</a>
<a class="twitter-btn">Twitter</a>
```

The SASS/CSS code required is this:

```
@mixin btn {
  border: thin solid #CCC;
  border-radius: 3px;
  padding: 5px;
  color: #FFF;
}
.facebook-btn {
  @include btn;
```

```
    background-color: #3b5998;
  }
  .twitter-btn {
    @include btn;
    background-color: #55acee;
  }
```

If you make use of the extend feature of CSS, which I would recommend as the processed CSS is a bit better, the code is as follows:

```
  .btn {
    border: thin solid #CCC;
    border-radius: 3px;
    padding: 5px;
    color: #FFF;
  }
  .facebook-btn {
    @extend .btn;
    background-color: #3b5998;
  }
  .twitter-btn {
    @extend .btn;
    background-color: #55acee;
  }
```

Let's now see the results of @include compared with @extend.

The results for @include are as follows:

```
  .facebook-btn {
    border: thin solid #CCC;
    border-radius: 3px;
    padding: 5px;
    color: #FFF;
    background-color: #3b5998;}

  .twitter-btn {
    border: thin solid #CCC;
    border-radius: 3px;
    padding: 5px;
    color: #FFF;
    background-color: #55acee;}
```

Here are the results for `@extend`:

```css
.btn, .twitter-btn, .facebook-btn {
  border: thin solid #CCC;
  padding: 5px;
  color: #FFF;
  border-radius: 3px; }

.facebook-btn {
  background-color: #3b5998; }

.twitter-btn {
  background-color: #55acee; }
```

When your CSS is compiled, all you need to use in your HTML is the `facebook-btn` and `twitter-btn` classes. All of the extension is done within your SASS, and you don't have to worry about cluttering your HTML with classes.

Suddenly, your CSS is even more maintainable and your HTML looks a lot neater. This information was taken from `http://www.smashingmagazine.com/2011/12/12/an-introduction-to-object-oriented-css-oocss/`.

Patterns and templates

Responsive design patterns are a great way to get your project started. There are plenty of resources on the web that you can use. One of my favorites is from Brad Frost at `http://bradfrost.github.io/this-is-responsive/patterns.html`.

It contains great patterns that have been optimized so that you can use them for your projects. I won't go into much detail about this as it is just meant to be a point of reference for you to start setting up your projects with some templates. There are a plenty of boilerplates available when using software such as Yeoman.

Media query templates

Using a base template for your media queries isn't a bad place to start with. There is a notion that media queries shouldn't be screen or device size-based. Instead, your media queries should be content-sensitive. Each of your projects will be different. Therefore, the breakpoints for each project will be different. A phrase I've often heard is as follows:

> *"Style your page until it looks good, then resize your browser until your site breaks or looks terrible, add a break point, and start again."*

I guess that, looking back at the content of this section, the heading might have been a bit deceiving. That said, templates and patterns are good to get your project going quickly but, in the end, each project will be unique.

Plugins and software

Constantly adding plugins to your project might actually be counter-intuitive. Essentially, you're trying to get rid of unnecessary downloads and code. Sometimes, however, there is a plugin you can add that actually helps achieve this.

Grunt

RequireJS is a JavaScript task runner. Now you might ask, "What is a JavaScript task runner?" Well, this is what the folks from Grunt have to say:

> *"In one word: automation. The less work you have to do when performing repetitive tasks like minification, compilation, unit testing, linting, etc, the easier your job becomes. After you've configured it through a Gruntfile, a task runner can do most of that mundane work for you – and your team – with basically zero effort."*

There is an entire slew of plugins that Grunt is compatible with. For a full list, take look at their plugin list page at `http://gruntjs.com/plugins`.

Ok, now let's take a look at how Grunt can help you save time and automate your work. You'll need to install grunt using `npm`. If you don't have `npm` installed, head over to `https://nodejs.org` and then download and install it.

Install Grunt by running the following code in your operating system's terminal or command line:

```
npm install -g grunt-cli
```

 Note that, if you are using a Unix-based system such as Mac OS X or Linux, you will have to run the command with the `sudo` prefix.

Generally, you will need to add at least two files to the root of your project. The first file, `package.json`, is used by `npm` to store metadata about your project and also to tell it which dependencies your project has.

`Gruntfile.js` is used to define tasks that `grunt` needs to run in the project.

package.json

The `package.json` file belongs to the root of your project, and needs to follow the specifications as defined at `https://docs.npmjs.com/files/package.json`.

Here is a simple example of a `package.json` file:

```
{
  "name": "my-project-name",
  "version": "0.1.0",
  "devDependencies": {
    "grunt": "~0.4.5",
    "grunt-contrib-jshint": "~0.10.0",
    "grunt-contrib-nodeunit": "~0.4.1",
    "grunt-contrib-uglify": "~0.5.0"
  }
}
```

Gruntfile.js

`Gruntfile.js` should be a valid JavaScript or CoffeeScript file that belongs to the root directory of your project.

The `Gruntfile` consists of the following parts:

- The wrapper function
- Your project and task configurations
- Loading Grunt plugins and tasks

Let's take a look at a basic example of a `Gruntfile`:

```
module.exports = function(grunt) {
  // Project configuration.
  grunt.initConfig({
    pkg: grunt.file.readJSON('package.json'),
    uglify: {
      options: {
        banner: '/*! <%= pkg.name %> <%=
grunt.template.today("yyyy-mm-dd") %> */\n'
      },
      build: {
        src: 'src/<%= pkg.name %>.js',
```

```
        dest: 'build/<%= pkg.name %>.min.js'
      }
    }
  });

  // Load the plugin that provides the "uglify" task
  grunt.loadNpmTasks('grunt-contrib-uglify');

  // Default task(s)
  grunt.registerTask('default', ['uglify']);

};
```

Going into more detail on this exceeds the scope of this book. Using programs such as Grunt is a great way to improve your productivity while developing and saves a lot of time.

RequireJS

One frustration that often exists is controlling which scripts get added to a page. You might not need all the scripts from your contact page to load into your home page. This is a source of over-downloading and fills up the network traffic with unnecessary requests.

A solution for this problem is a JavaScript module loader called RequireJS. It is optimized for in-browser use and can even run in other JavaScript environments such as Rhino and NodeJS.

RequireJS is even compatible with IE6 and later versions. You can download RequireJS from `http://requirejs.org/docs/download.html`.

The designers of the RequireJS module recommend that you keep all inline scripts out of your HTML code and carry out all of the script loading via RequireJS. So, your barebone index file might look something like the following.

Let's say your project structure looks as follows:

```
project-directory/
    index.html
    scripts/
        main.js
        require.js
        helper/
            util.js
```

This could be the `index.html` page's initial setup:

```
<html>
<head>
    <title>Hello RequireJS</title>
    <link href="css/awesome.css" rel="stylesheet" />
    <script data-main="js/main" src="js/require.js"></script></head>
<body>
    <h2>Hello RequireJS</h2>
    <p>Let's get those scripts 'a loadin'</p>
</body>
</html>
```

So, RequireJS is loading and, from there, it will handle the entire script loading as you configured. It's worth noting that you can also place the script included for RequireJS before the end of the `<body>` tag if you do not want it to block rendering of your page.

Let's see how we can configure RequireJS and make use of the optimization it offers:

```
require(["helper/util"], function(util) {
    //This function is called when scripts/helper/util.js is
    loaded.
    //If util.js calls define(), then this function is not fired
    until
    //util's dependencies have loaded, and the util argument will
    hold
    //the module value for "helper/util"
});
```

For more advanced script loading and to learn how to take full advantage of RequireJS take a look at its API documentation at `http://requirejs.org/docs/api.html`.

Summary

We focused on a few ways to improve our site. We started by looking at a design concept, graceful degradation, and progressive enhancement. We discussed the differences and how better user experience can be achieved on our website by making use of progressive enhancement rather than graceful degradation.

Making use of OOCSS can not only be of great benefit to your website's maintainability, it can also improve the loading speed. By following OOCSS, you can reduce the size of your CSS files, thereby improving the download time of the resources required to load your site. We also took a look at how we can improve OOCSS even further by combining it with a CSS preprocessor, such as SASS.

Patterns and templates were briefly mentioned, along with available patterns, to get you started with your project. As each project will be unique, your media queries will differ in order to achieve the results that you want.

Programs such as GruntJS and RequireJS can make your website more productive and improve your website's performance. GruntJS can automate Javascript tasks to save your time while you develop, and RequireJS is an excellent module loader for your JavaScript files.

8
Using Tools for Performance

When you start developing professionally, the time spent developing your projects is something that you should try to keep to a minimum. Less time means more projects, which means more profitability. When you have the correct tools, it can save valuable time.

We'll take a look at some of the most popular tools that are used across the Web and try and see how each product fits into our workflow. You should never be afraid to change your workflow, for the better of course.

Everyone has their preference when it comes to choosing a developing environment. Windows being the most popular, a lot of people get started on Windows and stay on it. Some people lean towards Mac OS X for its ease of use. Then there are those who are security-conscious, or perhaps firm believers in the open source community, and choose Linux. Linux also offers a good place to learn about server setup. Most modern hosting companies use Linux servers for PHP and HTML websites.

Now, for the most part, I'll mention cross-platform applications that you can use on Windows, Mac OS X, or Linux. In cases where there are no-cross platform options, I'll talk about similar products that you can use.

I'll break up the developing process into a few parts:

- Planning
- Developing
- Managing

Each of these topics has a toolset that is simple and reliable. Personal preference is the key factor here. No matter how I feel about a product, you may have a different outlook towards it.

Planning

The most crucial part of any project, and often overlooked, is planning. When you know exactly where your project is heading, following the road map is a piece of cake. Proper planning also helps you set realistic expectations for your clients.

When you develop a new site—a responsive site—it is important to sketch all possible layouts. The three form factors to consider, as we know, are desktop, tablet, and smartphone. If you've never heard of `http://www.interfacesketch.com/`, this is the time to go and check it out. This site supplies you with templates for a variety of tablets and smartphones and a web browser wireframe. These can be printed and used to start your mock-ups and make your planning a little easier. You can even download frames for specific models such as the iPhone 6 or Nexus 10 tablet. Here is a sample drawing of the iPhone 6:

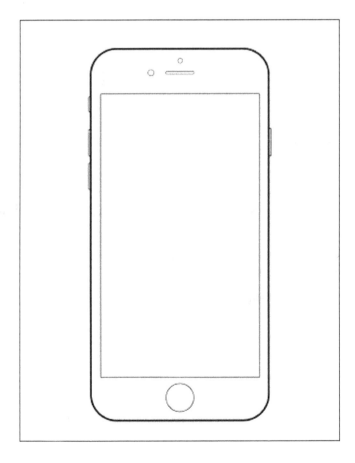

It's quite a simple thing—really. You can print it and start drawing your mock-ups immediately. Each project should have a collection of mock-ups, which are something to go back to once you get stuck.

The files are also in SVG format, so you can open them in Illustrator or Inkscape.

Of course, planning isn't just about drawing nice layouts. Planning consists of deadlines, taking notes, and being realistic about what can be achieved with the budget that is provided for the project.

A big part of planning is note taking. A favorite of mine that has been around for a while is Evernote. It's free, and it's also great! It is cross-platform, so you can view your notes on your desktop, tablet, phone, or simply a browser.

One interesting project I came across is `http://www.webflow.com`, a responsive website builder. I was quite skeptical in the beginning because I had never really come across a website builder that was particularly good. Webflow isn't bad at all! You can buy templates from their store, or just choose a blank template and start building your own. This is a great place to build a quick sample for your site. You can download the HTML and CSS when you're done.

Developing

There are countless options when it comes to typing your code. Some people prefer the distraction-free interfaces of Sublime Text or Notepad++, and others prefer powerful, full-fledged development solutions such as Jetbrains' Webstorm. As long as you are comfortable and know your way through your developing software, you'll be as productive as you can possibly be. Here is a list of some of the most popular text editors available:

- Brackets
- Sublime Text
- TextMate
- BBEdit
- Webstorm
- PHPStorm

Let's take a look at some all-in-one solutions. These are apps that can do all the wonderful things that web developers may need: minifying their CSS, concatenating their JavaScript files, and giving them the ability to preview their site on a multitude of devices on the same network, while they are developing their project.

CodeKit

CodeKit is an application that helps with everything you can think of when working on a project.

Minifiers, an SCSS processor, project dependency management, and live preview are all built into this application. CodeKit is available for Mac OS X only. Also, it's not a free application. If you really want a good-quality application that is maintained and has good support, paid apps are usually the way to go.

What makes CodeKit stand out? Well, take a look at this wonderful feature listing:

- **Preprocessor** : CodeKit has a preprocessor for SASS and LESS. Handy!

- **Compiling**: This simply means converting code into an understandable format for your web browser. As an example, your SASS code is compiled to become CSS with the help of a preprocessor.

- **Task Manager**: Your live browser refreshing is handled by a task manager. When you save a file, an event is triggered and the site is refreshed to reflect the new addition to your file.

- **Package Manager**: This is a great addition to CodeKit. You can open your project and choose from a list of up-to-date packages, from Bootstrap to jQuery, and the most popular packages you may want to use in your project. When an update is available, you can select your project and update the package right from CodeKit.

- **Minification**: You can minify your code in CodeKit, which saves the hassle of using separate applications for all your tasks.

- **Concatenation**: In programming, concatenation means combining two variable values into one. When we talk about file concatenation, however, it is slightly different. We've covered JavaScript file concatenation in *Chapter 5, The Fastest HTTP Request is No HTTP Request*.

- **CodeKit:** This allows you to decide which files are concatenated and in which order. Handy, I say!

There are a few free options available, such as npm with grunt. They are command-line-based and might be a bit more trouble to set up than just clicking a few buttons. You can download npm from `http://nodejs.org/`.

You can get a vast library of applications that are compatible with all versions of Windows, Mac OS X, and Linux, at `http://npm.org`.

Prepros

Another excellent tool that you can use is Prepros. It is cross-platform. Check it out at `https://prepros.io/`. It's not a free application but well worth the $29 that you pay for it. It is very similar to CodeKit, but there are some really cool extras.

Besides being cross-platform, it gives you the ability to set up live preview across your entire network. All you have to do is get a QR scanner app on your phone or tablet and scan the generated code. Voilà!

It has many of the features that CodeKit has and is a reliable option for managing your projects.

Some other options worth mentioning are as follows:

- **Grunt**: This is a command-line utility built on `node.js`
- **Gulp**: This is a command-line utility

Managing code changes

You're working on a project, you've made a big change, and something breaks. Then, you realize you don't have a backup of your project. I'm sure that has happened to many of us who have worked on big projects.

But then again, keeping track of changes and updates can become terribly tedious. So what to do? Well, version control is there to help. Some of the most popular ones are Git, Mercurial, and SVN.

Keeping your files synced across all your devices is also a pain. A simple solution if you don't want to make use of source control is to use something as simple as Dropbox, Google Drive, or even One Drive. All the aforementioned file accessing services are cross-compatible, so you can run them on Windows, Mac, or even Linux.

Now that you have taken care of the code management, you might find it increasingly difficult to keep track of your tasks at hand. Many tools exist for this purpose, and I feel Trello is a great experience. In it, you have the ability to create boards that can represent projects and share updates with your clients so they can see what you're up to. This is a web app and it's free.

Summary

This is a pretty introductory chapter at its roots. It was intended to point out the available applications that you can use to make your development better.

Now that we're almost done, we can just take a look at some resources to take what we've talked about further (see the Appendix). I'll mention a few great developers who have made significant contributions to the web field and give you some excellent starting points to further your knowledge of responsive web design.

Taking the Next Steps

We've covered a lot of things in this book and, from here, you'll need to go somewhere and expand your knowledge. In practice, you'll become a lot better at doing your job.

So where do you go from here?

The best approach from here is more reading, some more reading, and then some more reading!

I've learned that the more you read, the more you know, but you also realize how little you know. That shouldn't stop you from learning and becoming as good as you possibly can.

One of the things that help us become better is exploring, learning, and always trying out new things. Take responsive frameworks such as Bootstrap or Foundation for a spin, see how they work. You'll learn a lot by investigating other people's code. If you understand how things work, and work well, this will guide you in developing your own custom solutions. The best lessons learned are those that are learned while making mistakes yourself, or learning from others' mistakes, which can often save a lot of time.

The best approach from here is more reading, some more reading, and then some more reading!

An overview of what we've covered so far

Let's take a look at what we've covered up to this point.

We looked at some advantages and disadvantages of using responsive web design. Implementing it badly can result in a slow, underwhelming website that drives users away instead of keeping them clicking and happy.

In *Chapter 1, The Good, the Bad, and the Ugly of Responsive Web Design*, we talked about what responsive designing is and how it can make a difference to a website's accessibility and content representation. We also discussed why responsive designing came into being and what advantages or features it brought with it. We also saw how it can impact the end users' overall website experience.

In *Chapter 2, Tweaking Your Website for Performance*, we focused on ways to tweak the overall performance of your website, focusing on where to place resources in the DOM and DOM overloading, and briefly covered preloading. Placing scripts and style sheets in the correct places in your DOM can dramatically improve the overall load time and even user experience. Scripts that change the layout of your site should be placed at the top of the DOM in the `<head>` tags. The files that are not critical can easily be placed at the end of the DOM, just before the closing `<body>` tag, otherwise they will increase the load time. Scripts at the top — in the `<head>` tag — block the site from loading until the browser has downloaded those files. In contrast, if you place JavaScript files that affect the layout at the bottom of the DOM, just before the closing `<body>` tag, you might display to the user a mangled website that has not been formatted as per your code.

This chapter also briefly delved into content preloading using plugins such as CreateJS. Preloading content is a great way to have your site populated with the important bits before displaying it to the user. Another topic covered was DNS prefetching. This is a useful technique when your website accesses multiple sites that are on different domains. DNS prefetching attempts to resolve domain names before the user follows a link to that domain. If the domain has been resolved, the advantage of this will be that there is effectively no delay due to DNS name resolution.

The web is the master of images. *Chapter 3, Managing Images*, took this to heart as we focused on managing images on our website. We discussed the importance of choosing the correct format for the image on our website, and how each format differs. Optimizing images is crucial to performance. You will see on most website analyzers that image optimization is one of the main areas when it comes to reducing load time.

We talked about progressive images, conditional loading for images, and properly defining image size. This chapter also relooked at overpopulating the DOM with unnecessary elements. The chapter touched on how hidden elements in the DOM can slow down browsing experience, and proposed some solutions to overcome this problem. We also discussed the caching of images. This is a good way to decrease load time on your website. Your browser can save copies of images, style sheets, JavaScript, or even entire web pages.

Chapter 4, Learning Content Management, talked about managing the content of our site. This chapter had a lot of content and covered style sheets, media queries, and viewports. We also talked about background images with media queries and working with JavaScript.

This chapter also focused on the usage of Sassy CSS, or SASS, on your site. Even though this is not directly linked to increasing the performance of your site, it does increase your proficiency as a web developer. SASS supports complex functions that CSS simply does not offer. Variables alone make it a worthwhile expedition, for me.

We described how JavaScript can help ease the load time of our site. I mentioned AngularJS and gave a brief tutorial on using it to make a simple notes application. Next on the list was conditional loading. PHP also had an honorable mention, and then parallel downloads had the floor. One thing to keep in mind is that some browsers don't download JavaScript files in parallel, so spreading those files across multiple hosts may yield no benefits. You should not take JS files into consideration when allocating resources to multiple hosts.

We covered image scaling, explained why it is a bad idea, and suggested what you should do to avoid this.

In *Chapter 5, The Fastest HTTP Request is No HTTP Request*, we covered HTTP requests, boldly stating that the fastest HTTP request is no HTTP request. We discussed how sprite sheets can help remove unnecessary requests by combining certain images into a sprite sheet and not loading them one by one. Image framing using sprite sheets in `<image>` tags instead of background images was also discussed. The frame consists of a container element, a frame element, and the image element. This chapter also covered combining files to help reduce requests. The rest of the chapter focused on server-side optimization.

The next chapter, *Chapter 6, Testing, Testing, and Testing*, talked only about testing. The more you test, the less you have to fix at the end of your project. You also appear more professional and your clients are more satisfied. We discussed some web tools you can make use of to test the performance of your site. We also took a look at how waterfall charts work and how to use your browser's developer tools.

Chapter 7, Speeding Up Development with Design Concepts, Patterns, and Programs, covered the mobile-first principle and relooked at single-page application frameworks, such as AngularJS, as a solution for your web applications. Learning design concepts to enhance performance was the main purpose of this chapter. We took a look at how the mobile market has grown in recent years and how it has affected our job as web developers.

Chapter 8, Using Tools for Performance, covered tools for your development process. This wasn't directly related to responsive web design, but it was intended to make the road to getting your site up-and-running easier and faster. We looked at tools used to manage our projects and applications, help develop and test our websites, and keep our projects backed up with version control.

Finally, you're here, in *Appendix, Taking the Next Steps*. There is no road map that can take you to your destination of becoming an amazing web developer. The only thing you can do is read what others have to say. Learn how they approached common problems such as browser restrictions and non-cross-compatible features — the list is quite long. There are a plenty of developers who have made a lot of progress. Here is a list of a few developers whom I find very helpful and whom you should take note of.

A few references for further reading

Let's now go through a few references that we can resort to, if we need to dig deeper into the aforementioned concepts.

Ethan Marcotte

Ethan is the author of Responsive Web Design, and a pioneer in this field. In an earlier chapter, I did mention his book, and I can't emphasize enough that you have to go and give it a read.

Paul Irish

Paul Irish is an American frontend engineer and developer advocate for Google Chrome. He is also recognized as an expert in web technologies such as HTML5 and CSS3.

I'd say that pretty much sums it up. He has a site aptly named `http://www.paulirish.com`, so it is pretty easy to find his work.

Brad Frost

Another favorite developer of mine is Brad Frost. His website, `http://www.bradfrost.com`, is filled with wonderful advice and articles that are well worth a read. His topics of discussion include web design, writing, speaking, workshops, and consulting, just to name a few. His section on responsive design is filled with great patterns, resources, and news.

Ask the people who know

Inevitably, when you read, you will come across something that you don't fully understand. This is when you go looking for people who have been familiar with that subject for a long time. You'll notice that the community is very willing to help and assist. Asking questions on active forums often produces sufficient results.

Summary

Okay, so that's it! You should now be well on your way to becoming a world-class developer. This book is intended to lay a foundation for you to get started and get a better idea on how to improve the speed of your responsive website. There is so much more that can be said about responsive design—some things were not even covered.

You should take the knowledge you gained, proceed with it, and add your own flavor. Read about what other people are doing to improve their websites and bring it all together.

Index

Package Manager 126
preprocessor 126
Task Manager 126
file concatenation 92
files
  combining 89
fonts 72, 73

G

graceful degradation 106-108
Grunt
  about 117
  URL 117
Gruntfile.js 118
Gzip compression test
  reference link 91

H

h5bp/html5-boilerplate
  reference link 90
HAML 59

I

image format
  selecting 31, 32
image framing 81-88
ImageOptim
  URL 32
images
  optimizing 32
Initializr
  URL 89
Interface Sketch
  URL 124

J

JavaScript
  used, for speeding up website 68
JPEGMini
  URL 32

L

LESS
  code 66, 67

references 66
LoadQueue function
  supported file types 25

M

management perspective, responsive
    web design
  benefits 5
media queries
  about 58, 67, 68
  specifying 51, 52
media query templates 116
minification 7
mobile first approach
  reference link 105
Mozilla Developers Network docs
  reference link 52

N

npm
  URL, for downloading 126

O

object-oriented CSS (OOCSS)
  about 109
  and SASS/SCSS 113-116
  containers, separating 111, 112
  content, separating 111, 112
  reference link 116
  structure, separating from styling 109, 110
one-to-many DOM elements 30, 44-51

P

package.json file
  about 118
  reference link 118
parallel downloads 70
patterns
  about 116
  reference link 116
pixels 72
planning 124, 125
plugins 117

results, assessing 99
testing 99
testing tools
reference link 104
TinyPNG
URL 32

U

Unresponsive Interactions 7

V

viewports 58

W

W3C spec, for media queries
reference link 58
Webflow
about 125
URL 125
WebPageTest
URL 101

Y

Yeoman
URL 89
URL, for generators' page 90
YSlow 13
YUI Compressor
reference link 92

Thank you for buying
Responsive Design High Performance

About Packt Publishing

Packt, pronounced 'packed', published its first book, *Mastering phpMyAdmin for Effective MySQL Management*, in April 2004, and subsequently continued to specialize in publishing highly focused books on specific technologies and solutions.

Our books and publications share the experiences of your fellow IT professionals in adapting and customizing today's systems, applications, and frameworks. Our solution-based books give you the knowledge and power to customize the software and technologies you're using to get the job done. Packt books are more specific and less general than the IT books you have seen in the past. Our unique business model allows us to bring you more focused information, giving you more of what you need to know, and less of what you don't.

Packt is a modern yet unique publishing company that focuses on producing quality, cutting-edge books for communities of developers, administrators, and newbies alike. For more information, please visit our website at www.packtpub.com.

About Packt Open Source

In 2010, Packt launched two new brands, Packt Open Source and Packt Enterprise, in order to continue its focus on specialization. This book is part of the Packt Open Source brand, home to books published on software built around open source licenses, and offering information to anybody from advanced developers to budding web designers. The Open Source brand also runs Packt's Open Source Royalty Scheme, by which Packt gives a royalty to each open source project about whose software a book is sold.

Writing for Packt

We welcome all inquiries from people who are interested in authoring. Book proposals should be sent to author@packtpub.com. If your book idea is still at an early stage and you would like to discuss it first before writing a formal book proposal, then please contact us; one of our commissioning editors will get in touch with you.

We're not just looking for published authors; if you have strong technical skills but no writing experience, our experienced editors can help you develop a writing career, or simply get some additional reward for your expertise.

[PACKT] open source ✣
PUBLISHING   community experience distilled

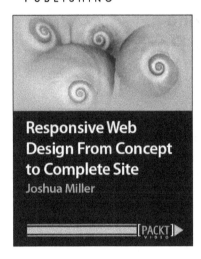

Responsive Web Design From Concept to Complete Site [Video]

ISBN: 978-1-78216-570-5   Duration: 02:04 hours

Easily design responsive websites that can adapt to any device regardless of screen size using HTML 5 and CSS3

1. Learn how to create fluid styles that flow to fill a browser of any size.

2. Discover the best design and coding practices in HTML5 and CSS3 for flexible layouts.

3. Contains everything you need to know to create simple to complex responsive sites starting from a design mockup to implementing it as a finished product.

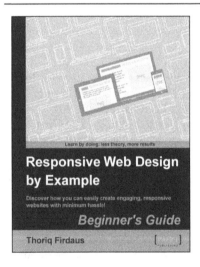

Responsive Web Design by Example Beginner's Guide

ISBN: 978-1-84969-542-8   Paperback: 338 pages

Discover how you can easily create engaging, responsive websites with minimum hassle!

1. Rapidly develop and prototype responsive websites by utilizing powerful open source frameworks.

2. Focus less on the theory and more on results, with clear step-by-step instructions, previews, and examples to help you along the way.

3. Learn how you can utilize three of the most powerful responsive frameworks available today: Bootstrap, Skeleton, and Zurb Foundation.

Please check **www.PacktPub.com** for information on our titles

Responsive Web Design with HTML5 and CSS3

ISBN: 978-1-84969-318-9   Paperback: 324 pages

Learn responsive design using HTML5 and CSS3 to adapt websites to any browser or screen size

1. Everything needed to code websites in HTML5 and CSS3 that are responsive to every device or screen size.

2. Learn the main new features of HTML5 and use CSS3's stunning new capabilities including animations, transitions and transformations.

3. Real world examples show how to progressively enhance a responsive design while providing fall backs for older browsers.

HTML5 and CSS3 Responsive Web Design Cookbook

ISBN: 978-1-84969-544-2   Paperback: 204 pages

Learn the secrets of developing responsive websites capable of interfacing with today's mobile Internet devices

1. Learn the fundamental elements of writing responsive website code for all stages of the development lifecycle.

2. Create the ultimate code writer's resource using logical workflow layers.

3. Full of usable code for immediate use in your website projects.

4. Written in an easy-to-understand language giving knowledge without preaching.

Please check **www.PacktPub.com** for information on our titles